Law Essentia

FAMILY LAW

Law Essentials

FAMILY LAW

Kenneth McK. Norrie, LL.B., Ph.D., F.R.S.E.

Professor of Law, University of Strathclyde

DUNDEE UNIVERSITY PRESS
2006

First published in Great Britain in 2006 by
Dundee University Press
University of Dundee
Dundee DD1 4HN

www.dundee.ac.uk/dup

ISBN 1–84586–011–X
EAN 978–1–84586–011–0

No natural forests were destroyed to make this product;
only farmed timber was used and replanted.

British Library Cataloguing-in-Publication Data
A catalogue record for this book is available on request from the British Library

Typeset by Waverley Typesetters, Little Walsingham, Norfolk
Printed and bound by Bell & Bain Ltd, Glasgow

CONTENTS

TABLE OF CASES

TABLE OF STATUTES

1 LEGAL PERSONALITY

Family law is primarily the law of natural persons and, as such, a number of issues need to be examined before moving onto the major part of the discipline, which is how the law regulates personal relationships between natural persons. The concept of natural person requires us to examine (i) the nature and acquisition of legal personality; (ii) age; and (iii) gender.

Nature and acquisition of legal personality

Legal personality is the concept whereby a "person" is recognised as existing by the law in a juridically active sense: in other words as an entity that can perform juridical acts such as entering into contracts, suing and being sued, and owning and dealing with property. Without legal personality an entity can be no more than the subject of legal rights and responsibilities – it cannot be the holder thereof. A building, an animal or a tree has no legal personality and so cannot own property, enter contracts or be sued. A limited liability company or other incorporated body, on the other hand, does have legal personality and so can be the holder of legal rights and responsibilities; and so too, in a system that eschews slavery, will every natural human person. Legal personality in this sense is acquired by natural persons at the moment of live birth. Before then, while there exists an entity that might be entitled to legal protection, that entity is not entitled to own property, to sue or be sued, or to enter into contracts. To deny the child before birth legal personality is not to deny that anything exists or is recognised by the law: it merely denies their power to own property etc. The law of abortion, for example, recognises the existence of the child before birth and provides protection from unlawful abortion: but that is very different from saying the child before birth has legal personality. Rather, the unborn child is like a listed building: it exists in the physical world and is protected by the law to the extent that before it can be destroyed various permissions are demanded. The present law of abortion in Scotland is a mixture of common law and statute. The common law prohibits it as a crime, and statute (the Abortion Act 1967, as amended by the Human Fertilisation and Embryology Act 1990) provides a potential accused with various defences to the criminal charge. These are as follows:

(i) that the continuation of the pregnancy would involve risk, greater than if the pregnancy were terminated, of injury to the physical or mental health of the pregnant woman or any existing children of her family (this ground being available only during the first 24 weeks of pregnancy);

(ii) that the termination is necessary to prevent grave permanent injury to the physical or mental health of the pregnant woman (no time limit);

(iii) that the continuation of the pregnancy would involve risk to the life of the pregnant woman, greater than if the pregnancy were terminated (no time limit);

(iv) that there is a substantial risk that if the child were born it would suffer from such physical or mental abnormalities as to be seriously handicapped (no time limit).

However, it should be noted that these defences need exist only in the mind of the accused, and *not* in fact. So a prosecutor must show (and remember that as a criminal charge it must be shown beyond reasonable doubt) that the accused did not believe in good faith that any of the above circumstances existed. It is nothing to the point whether or not, for example, the woman's life was really at any risk.

The child before birth is also entitled to be protected from harm short of destruction, and the source of this harm is often the mother. It is not, however, possible to take action against the mother (such as locking her up) to prevent her from, for example, taking drugs that will harm her child. But behaviour of a pregnant woman during pregnancy can be used to justify removing the child after it is born if this behaviour indicates that the woman or her lifestyle will continue to harm the child after birth.

The child before birth is recognised as existing for other purposes even without the attribution of legal personality. It was accepted in Roman law and remains the case today that a posthumous child is entitled to succession rights. So if, for example, a father dies before his child is born, that child will be entitled to claim a share in his succession. This is known as the *nasciturus* principle. Its application is, however, subject to two conditions: first, the claim must be to a direct benefit and not indirect, for example traced through another person, and, second, the child must be subsequently born alive. Another requirement, flowing from s 28(6) of the Human Fertilisation and Embryology Act 1990, is that the embryo that grows into the child must begin so to grow during the life of the father. The statute uses the less than obvious language of the father's sperm, or the embryo created with his sperm, being "used" before his death, but the meaning is fairly clear. If a man's sperm is used to create an embryo during his life, or if the embryo so created is implanted into a woman during his life, then any subsequent child created using his sperm is in law his and succession rights arise, but if the child is created with his sperm used for *not* ? that purpose after his death he is for no purpose of law the father. > but in fact ?

Age

A person's age is crucial to the law for that person's status, and age is counted from the beginning of the day upon which the person is born. So a person becomes 16 at the beginning of the 16th anniversary of his or her birth (Age of Legal Capacity (Scotland) Act 1991, s 6). There is in Scotland no single age at which a person moves from childhood to adulthood. Rather, it depends entirely upon the issue, and the so-called "age of majority" (which is 18) is virtually limited in terms of legal consequence to the age of voting. Twelve is the crucial age for making a will and consenting to adoption; 16 is the age of marriage, lawful heterosexual intercourse with a girl, lawful gay (male) sex, and the escaping from parental rights; 18 is the age at which young persons can vote. There are various other statutory ages dealing with matters such as driving a car, joining the army, being employed, leaving school etc. Additionally, there are certain juridical activities at which no specified age is laid down for everyone: rather, the law treats each individual separately and determines on a case by case basis whether the young person is old enough to do this or that. Entering into legal transactions (typically contracts) is the most important example, for the Age of Legal Capacity (Scotland) Act 1991, s 2(1) provides that a person under the age of 16 can do this so long as (i) it is of a type that is not uncommon in that person's age and circumstances and (ii) its terms and conditions are not unreasonable. Another example is giving consent to medical treatment, which can be done by a person under the age of 16 so long as he or she understands (in the view of the health care professional providing the treatment) the nature and possible consequences of the treatment (1991 Act, s 2(4)). Children who do not have capacity for either of these acts will need to have them carried out on their behalf by their "legal representatives".

Gender

Modern society continues to be gendered both socially and legally. Socially we continue to expect individuals' places and roles to be determined by their gender; legally the law still requires certain activities to be carried out by one gender rather than the other. The most obvious example of this in Family Law is marriage and civil partnership: the former can be contracted only by two persons who are of the opposite sex to each other, the latter can be contracted only by two persons who are of the same sex as each other. So how does the law define whether a person is male or female?

For most people this is a matter that is both obvious and unambiguous. For at least two categories, however, the issue raises serious doubts. First there are individuals who are born with mixed gender characteristics: the so-called intersex persons. There are a variety of medical syndromes and chromosomal abnormalities which lead to individuals possessing characteristics of both sexes. Though there has been little discussion of the matter in Scotland, such little authority as we have suggests that a "predominance" approach has to be taken to classify such individuals as either "male" or "female". By this is meant that the various factors that normally all point in the same direction (chromosomes, hormones, gonads, genitalia, self-perception, social role) are weighted and the person is deemed male or female by whichever is predominant. And if a mistake is made at birth because, for example, only external appearance is taken into account, then this can be corrected later.

Second, there are individuals whose physical characteristics, both external and internal, are clearly of one gender but their brain tells them irresistibly that they are of the other gender. Such people are called transsexuals, transgender people or "trans people". For many decades now it has been possible to ameliorate the immense distress this disjunction of body and mind causes by hormonal and surgical treatment designed to make the individual's body look more like the gender their mind tells them they belong to. But until recently the law was rigid in defining a person's gender as that which was physically presented at birth. Put simply, "sex change" was not legally possible.

However, this position was reversed after the European Court of Human Rights held it to be incompatible with the European Convention on Human Rights, as a breach of both Article 8 (right to private life) and Article 12 (right to marry). The UK Government responded with the Gender Recognition Act 2004 which set up a Gender Recognition Panel. This Panel, on the basis of evidence presented before it, is able to determine that an applicant who used to be of one gender is now of the opposite gender. If this determination is made then the Panel will grant a "gender recognition certificate" and that amounts to a change of the legal sex of the applicant, for all purposes of law including, crucially, marriage and civil partnership.

Essential Facts

- Legal personality begins at the moment of live birth.
- Abortion is a crime but medical practitioners have various defences.
- An unborn child will be treated as being in life whenever this is to its direct advantage.
- A child created through the use of a dead man's sperm has no legal father.
- A person's gender is initially determined by biological criteria, though it can be lawfully changed by the acquisition of a gender recognition certificate.

Essential Cases

Cox's Trs v Cox (1950). Mr Charles Cox was a wealthy solicitor in Banchory. When he died he left his property to the descendants (children, grandchildren etc) of his four brothers and his sister. Four such descendants were born after Mr Cox's death, but had been *in utero* at the date of death.

The court applied the *nasciturus* principle that an unborn child will be treated as born whenever it is to the unborn child's advantage, and so the unborn descendants were entitled to share the legacy.

Elliot v Joicey (1935). A legacy was to be divided amongst certain named children. If any predeceasing child had died childless their share was to go to the other named children; if any predeceasing child had died survived by children of their own their share was to remain in their estate (for distribution to their own children). One child predeceased leaving a child *in utero*.

The court held that the *nasciturus* principle, under which a child *in utero* will be treated as being in life, only applied when it was of direct benefit to the unborn child and that in this case the benefit did not directly accrue to the unborn child but to the estate of its parent (the testator's child). So the predeceasing (testator's) child was held to have died childless.

Re F (In Utero) (1988). A pregnant woman who was inadequate was considered to be adopting a mode of life unsuitable for a child: she was inconsistent, had no fixed address, dabbled in drugs and was sometimes to be found wandering around Turkey. The local authority sought to have the unborn child made a ward of court.

The court held that this was not possible. To protect the unborn child from a feckless mother could only be done by interfering with the rights and freedoms of the mother, which was unjustified.

D (A Minor) v Berkshire County Council (1987). A child was born suffering from drug withdrawal symptoms and had been removed from the care of its parents immediately on birth: the ground for removal was that the child "was being harmed" by the parents. The parents argued that since the child had been removed immediately on birth they never had the chance to harm the child.

The court held that the child was being harmed by the mother before birth by her taking of drugs and therefore could be removed from the parents, even before they had been given an opportunity to show whether they would look after the child properly.

Re MB (1997). A woman who was about to give birth to a child was advised that she needed to have a Caesarean section for the good of the child. She refused because she had a needle phobia. The Health Authority sought a court order permitting them to perform the operation without her consent.

The Court of Appeal held that an adult competent patient had an absolute right to refuse consent to medical treatment, for good reason or bad, or no reason at all. Operations without consent can be performed only when the patient lacks mental competence. In this case the woman's needle phobia took away her power of rational thought and so she was held to be incompetent. The operation was ordered. (*Quaere*: does being in labour reduce a woman's capacity to make rational decisions any more than a needle phobia, with the result that the medical profession takes over her decision-making powers?)

Kelly v Kelly (1997). Mr and Mrs Kelly separated and they were in the process of divorce when it became known that Mrs Kelly was pregnant. Mr Kelly was the father but Mrs Kelly decided to seek an abortion. Mr Kelly objected and he sought an interdict to prevent her from going through with the termination. He claimed that he had title as the child's guardian and also in his own right.

The court held that a fetus has no "right" to remain in the mother's womb and so, if the abortion were carried out lawfully under the Abortion Act 1967, there would be no legally recognised loss that could be prevented by interdict.

Paton v UK (1981). Mr Paton, like Mr Kelly, failed in his attempt in the UK courts to prevent his wife from aborting their child. He claimed this was an infringement of his article 8 right to family life and of the unborn child's Article 2 right to life.

The European Court dismissed his claim: the interference in his right to family life was justified by the need to protect the rights of the mother; the Article 2 right is impliedly limited in the early stages of pregnancy in order to protect the life and health of the woman.

2 CREATING THE PARENT–CHILD RELATIONSHIP

The parent–child relationship comes into existence, in its fullest sense, when the child is born. The vast majority of children are born as a result of an act of sexual intercourse between their parents, but a growing number of children are conceived by other means, such as artificial insemination, in vitro fertilisation or embryo transfer. The legal parent–child relationship does not always reflect the genetic connection between the child and the producer of the sperm and egg from which he or she was created. This is so even when the child is born as a result of sexual intercourse.

Creation through sexual intercourse

When a child has been born as a result of sexual intercourse between a man and a woman the law deems the mother to be the woman who conceives with her eggs and gives birth to the child, and it presumes the father to be either (i) the man who is married to the mother at the moment of birth (or was married to her at any time between conception and birth) or (ii) the man who has acknowledged the child as his and who is registered in the Register of Births as the father of the child (Law Reform (Parent and Child) (Scotland) Act 1986, s 5). The presumption of paternity is rebuttable, by proof on the balance of probabilities either that the mother's husband is not, or that some other man is, the genetic father of the child. In cases of doubt this is usually fairly easily established by means of a DNA test on both the child and the man alleged to be (or not to be) the father. But until the presumption is rebutted in a court of law the husband will be treated for all purposes as the father of the child, even when in fact he is not. If the mother is not married, and no man is registered as the father, the child is *not* legally fatherless: rather there is no man who is presumed to be the father. But paternity can be established in the same way as the presumption of paternity can be rebutted, that is to say by evidence on the balance of probabilities.

Creation through infertility treatment

When a woman becomes pregnant through some form of infertility treatment, the law deems her to be the mother when she gives birth to the child (Human Fertilisation and Embryology Act 1990, s 27): this is so even when she has no genetic link to the child (for example when she becomes pregnant through implantation in her of an embryo created with another woman's egg). So the woman who gives birth to the child is, for all purposes, the mother of that child. Sometimes infertility treatment involves using sperm from a donor, and in that situation the law will deem the mother's partner (if she has one, and he is male) to be the father of the child. The application of this rule is slightly different depending upon whether the mother is married to her partner or not. If she is married to her partner, then the man is deemed to be the father of the child unless it can be shown that he did not consent to the infertility treatment that led to her becoming pregnant (1990 Act, s 28(2)). If she is not married to her partner, then the man is deemed to be the father of the child if the infertility treatment has been provided to the woman and the man "together" (1990 Act, s 28(3)). In the latter situation, however, there is an additional requirement, which is that the treatment must have been provided in the course of licensed treatment provided by a provider authorised to do so by the Human Fertilisation and Embryology Authority. The effect of this extra qualification is that "do-it-yourself" insemination of an unmarried woman does not confer paternity on her partner; the fact that this extra qualification does not apply to married couples means that "do-it-yourself" insemination of a married woman does confer paternity on her husband (unless it is shown that he did not consent). In either situation paternity cannot be removed from the mother's partner by showing that he has no genetic link, or that another man does have a genetic link, to the child, for the rules only apply when the partner has no such link. The donor of the sperm (and the man who does have the genetic link) is in law not the father if the donation was to a licensed clinic and he consented to his donation being used for the creation of a child.

There are two situations in which a child born through infertility treatment will be deemed to be legally fatherless. The first is when the donor of the sperm has had his paternity cut off by the application of the above rule but the woman has no male partner who can be deemed father; the second is when the sperm or the embryo created with the sperm was "used" after the death of the provider of the sperm. "Used" means used to bring about a pregnancy. This second situation is designed to deal with the long-term storage of sperm or embryos, for during the period of storage the provider of the sperm may die. If that happens the winding up of that dead man's estate would otherwise have to be postponed until all his sperm, or embryos created with his sperm, had been used up. But even although the child is legally fatherless for practical purposes, it is possible to register the dead man as the father, so long as it can be shown that he consented to this happening.

Creation through court order

A parent–child relationship can be created through court order in two situations: a so-called "parental order" after a surrogacy arrangement (governed by s 30 of the Human Fertilisation and Embryology Act 1990) and, more commonly, an adoption order (governed by the Adoption (Scotland) Act 1978 or the Adoption and Children (Scotland) Bill 2006 (being debated as this book goes to press)).

A parental order may be applied for by a married couple who have commissioned a third party to bear a child for them, with the third party agreeing to give up the child, once born, to the commissioning couple. The couple must apply for the order within six months of the birth of the child, one or other of them must be the genetic parent of the child, the surrogate mother must not have been paid a fee (though reasonable expenses are permitted) and she must freely consent to the making of the order. If the surrogate mother refuses to part with the child once it is born then there is nothing the commissioning couple can do about it, and if the child has been given up but the surrogate mother refuses to consent to the parental order, again there is nothing that can be done. She is the mother, since she is the one who gave birth to the child.

To a large extent the parental order and its effects mirror the rules for adoption, though these are much more complex. The key to understanding adoption is to recognise that the adoption order does two things: it creates a parent–child relationship and, by definition, it also destroys the existing parent–child relationship. The latter effect is the main motivation for most adoptions today, which is therefore an aspect of the child-care and protection system which comes into operation when the existing parent–child relationship is operating in a manner that is detrimental to the interests of the child. This is discussed further in Chapter 5 below.

There are rules governing who may be adopted and who may adopt. In Scots law only a child may be adopted, and this is defined to mean for this purpose a person under the age of 18 years (though it is now possible for the order to be made after the person's 18th birthday if the process began before that date). If the child is over 12 years old then his or her consent is necessary and without that consent the adoption cannot go ahead – the child has an absolute veto. The child must be at least 19 weeks old and have lived with the prospective adopters at all times during the preceding 13 weeks if the adopter is a relative or the child has been placed with the adopter by an adoption agency; otherwise the child must be one year old at the time of the making of the ordert. Under the 1978 Act only a married couple may adopt jointly, but the 2006 Bill, as published, will permit unmarried couples in "enduring family relationships" to adopt; and civil partners too will be permitted to adopt. A single person may adopt a child, and a married person or civil partner may not adopt other than jointly with his or her spouse, unless the spouse cannot be found or is incapable through ill-health of adopting, or the spouses are permanently separated.

Given that the adoption order will destroy the existing parent–child relationship, it can be made only if the existing parents either agree to the adoption or, having forfeited or lost the right to prevent the child's welfare being advanced by the order, have had their agreement dispensed with by the court. The grounds for dispensing with the parents' agreement (Adoption (Scotland) Act 1978, s 16) are as follows:

(a) that the parent is not known, cannot be found or is incapable of agreeing;
(b) that the parent is withholding agreement unreasonably;
(c) that the parent has persistently failed to fulfil parental responsibilities;
(d) that the parent has seriously ill-treated the child.

If one or more of these grounds exists the court must then decide whether it is in the interests of the child that parental agreement should be dispensed with. Under the 2006 Bill grounds (b), (c) and (d) are replaced with a new ground: that the welfare of the child requires parental consent to be dispensed with.

Once the appropriate consents and agreements have been obtained the court will appoint various officers to examine the case, interview the child and prospective parents and take account of the reports these officers produce in deciding whether to make an adoption order. The paramount consideration for making the order is the welfare of the child (1978 Act, s 6), though the adoption agency must also explore the extent to which an order less severe than an adoption order will achieve the purpose of securing the welfare of the child.

An adoption order, once made, is (subject only to the normal appeal process) final and irrevocable, except in limited circumstances such as when the order has been obtained by fraud or was made incompetently (for example over an adult).

Essential Facts

- A child's father is presumed to be the man who is either married to the mother or is registered as the father.
- When a child is born to a married woman after infertility treatment, the mother's husband is deemed to be the father unless he did not consent to the treatment.
- When a child is born to an unmarried woman after infertility treatment, the mother's partner (if male) is deemed to be the father if the treatment is provided to both together.
- A "parental order" transfers parenthood from a surrogate mother to a commissioning (married) couple.
- An adoption order destroys the parenthood of the birth parents and creates parenthood in the adopters.
- A child of 12 or more must consent before an adoption order is made.

Essential Cases

Leeds Teaching Hospital NHS Trust v A & Ors (2003). After infertility treatment a white couple gave birth to a child who was clearly of mixed race. Investigation established that there had been a mixup at the infertility clinic and that the sperm of a black man (who with his wife was also undergoing infertility treatment at the same clinic) had been mixed up with that of the white man. Who was the father of the child? The matter turned on the interpretation of 28(2) of the Human Fertilisation and Embryology Act 1990, which provides that the husband of a woman who becomes pregnant as a result of infertility treatment is the father, unless it can be shown that he did not consent to the treatment.

The court held that the white man had not consented to his wife being impregnated with the sperm of the black man therefore he was not the father. Since the Act did not provide the answer, genetics did so and the black man was the father. The parties, good people all, had previously agreed that the child should remain with the white couple: the case might have been substantially more difficult had the black couple sought possession of what the court declared to be the black man's child.

Evans v Amicus Healthcare Ltd (2004). Ms Natallie Evans and Mr Howard Johnston were a couple attempting to have a child via infertility treatment. Embryos were created with the sperm of Mr Johnston and the eggs of Ms Evans (who could thereafter produce no more). Before they were implanted into Ms Evans the couple separated and Mr Johnston withdrew his consent to the embryos being used for the purpose of creating babies. Ms Evans sought to have this rule declared a breach of her right to found a family.

The court held that she did not have a right to found a family in circumstances which imposed family life on another person against his wishes. Any right she had to use the embryos was no stronger than Mr Johnston's right to refuse to allow them to be used. She could, in any case, still become a mother by using another woman's eggs and finding another man. The European Court of Human Rights agreed

In Re D (2005). A woman, Ms D, and a man, Mr B, were not married to each other but were undergoing infertility treatment together. Embryos were created with Ms D's eggs and donor sperm and a series of attempts at implantation commenced. The first attempt in October 1998 failed but the second attempt in May 1999 was successful. But in March 1999 the couple's relationship had terminated. Ms D had not informed the clinic of this fact. When the child was born Mr B sought a contact order and parental responsibility over the child. Ms D denied that he was the father.

Section 28(3) of the Human Fertilisation and Embryology Act 1990 deems the male partner in an unmarried (heterosexual) relationship to be the father if treatment is provided to the couple "together". Mr B argued that the time to test this was the time when the embryos were created (at which point the relationship still existed); Ms D argued that the time to test this was when the embryos were implanted. The House of Lords agreed with Ms D. The result was that Mr B was not deemed to be the father and he had no title to seek contact or parental responsibility.

C v S (1996). Mr and Mrs C agreed with Ms S that Ms S would be artificially inseminated with Mr C's sperm, become pregnant, bear a child and give up the child to Mr and Mrs C on its birth, on the understanding that the couple would seek a parental order under the Human Fertilisation and Embryology Act 1990 and the mother would agree (as was required by that Act). The price was £8,000. The child was born, the money was paid, and the birth was registered by Ms S naming Mr C as the father. Mr and Mrs C took the child home. Ms S then changed her mind and wanted her child back. Mr and Mrs C applied to adopt the child. The sheriff held that the payment of £8,000 contravened the Adoption (Scotland) Act 1978 and also the Human Fertilisation and Embryology Act 1990 and so he could make no order under either Act. But he made a residence order in favour of Mr and Mrs C and refused contact with Ms S.

On appeal the Court of Session held that the sheriff had been wrong to hold himself unable to make an adoption order: the £8,000 had been paid for the mother to consent to a parental order but not an adoption order and so there was no contravention of the Adoption (Scotland) Act. The adoption order was made in favour of Mr and Mrs C.

Re B (Adoption Order: Jurisdiction to set aside) (1995). A young man who had been adopted as a child by a Jewish couple sought to have the adoption order revoked after the death of his adoptive parents, on the basis that they had been defrauded into adopting him by having been told that he was Jewish when in fact he was an Arab.

The court dismissed this claim and held that only in the most exceptional circumstances could a court revoke an adoption order, such as deliberate and bad faith fraud which did not exist in this case.

T, Petitioner (1997). The petitioner sought to adopt a child who had very special needs. He was a gay man living in a stable relationship with a partner who would share in the upbringing of the child. The child's mother refused to have anything to do with the process (or the child). No one objected to the petitioner's care for the child nor his application. At first instance, however, the judge found that as a matter of principle gay men should not be permitted to adopt children.

On appeal, the Inner House overturned this decision and said that the only matter of principle was the welfare of the child: in the instant case it was clearly best for the child to be adopted by the man who was bringing it up. Though the Adoption (Scotland) Act 1978 prevented his partner joining in the application, the Act did not prevent a gay man in these circumstances from adopting.

L v Central Regional Council (1990). Central Regional Council sought an order freeing two children for adoption. Their mother had given them up into local council care because she could not cope with them, but she wanted to remain their mother. She did not maintain regular access with the children.

The Court of Session held that in determining whether to dispense with parental consent the court had to adopt a two-stage test. (1) Was there a ground for dispensing? This is a matter of fact and in the present case there was lack of parental care which was a ground. (2) Is it in the interests of the child to dispense with parental agreement and so allow the adoption? This is a matter of judgement on the part of the court and in the present case it was in the interests of the children to be adopted.

3 BRINGING UP CHILDREN

Children have a right to be brought up by their parents, as defined by their own legal system (UN Convention on the Rights of the Child, Art 7), and both parents and children have a right to respect for their family life (European Convention on Human Rights, Art 8). By and large, parents are left free to determine how best to bring up their children, but there are numerous duties that parents must fulfil, because the essence of the parent–child relationship is one of parental responsibility to bring up children properly: it ought not to be seen (though it often is) as one that confers rights on parents to bring up children the way they think fit. Parents are, however, for the most part, left to do just that. The law lays down a set of minimum standards, and failure to meet these standards will usually justify the state stepping in for the benefit of the child. These standards are contained in various statutes, such as the Children (Scotland) Act 1995, which sets out in fairly general terms the parental responsibilities and parental rights that the law imposes on parents, the Family Law (Scotland) Act 1985, which governs the obligation of parents to aliment (ie to provide financially for the child), and the various Education (Scotland) Acts which govern the obligations on parents to educate their children.

Who is obliged to fulfil upbringing duties?

Because the various obligations imposed on parents are contained in different statutes, the person subject to these obligations is defined in each, and is defined differently.

(a) Parental responsibilities and parental rights (Children (Scotland) Act 1995)

The responsibility and right to make decisions as to how a child is to be brought up are imposed not on all "parents", however defined, but only on (i) mothers and (ii) fathers who are registered as such in the Register of Births. They may also be imposed on other persons (including unregistered fathers) if a parent nominates that person to be the child's guardian after the death of the parent, or if a court makes an order imposing parental responsibilities and parental rights on such a person, or if the mother agrees to share them with the father. The court must be

motivated by the welfare of the child, but a parent or guardian making a
will or an agreement does not need to be.

(b) Aliment (Family Law (Scotland) Act 1985)

All parents legally defined as such, whether married to each other or
not, or registered in the Register of Births or not, or living with the
child or not, are obliged to maintain the child in a financial sense. The
obligation of aliment is extended beyond parents and is imposed also
on any person who has accepted the child as a member of his or her
family even though he or she is not actually the parent of the child. So
the step-parent or co-parent who has accepted the child as a member
of his or her family is obliged to the same extent as the actual parent to
aliment the child.

(c) Education (Education (Scotland) Act 1981)

Again all parents are obliged to ensure that their children receive an
efficient education, and again the obligation is extended beyond parents
to include any person who has an obligation to maintain the child. So
those obliged under this Act are the same as the people obliged under the
provisions relating to aliment.

(d) Other

There are some other obligations that are imposed on persons who
happen to have children in their actual care even although they do not
have a parent–child relationship (such as, typically, step-parents). Any
person who has care or control of a child is obliged to protect the welfare
of that child (Children (Scotland) Act 1995, s 5) and in particular may
provide consent to the child's medical treatment. Similarly, any person
who has in fact charge of, or control over, a child is obliged to attend
with the child at any children's hearing arranged in respect of that child
(Children (Scotland) Act 1995, s 93, definition of "relevant person" for
the purposes of the children's hearing system).

Parental responsibilities and parental rights

Section 1 of the Children (Scotland) Act 1995 sets out the parental
responsibilities that govern parents in their bringing up of children.
These are as follows:

   (a) the responsibility to safeguard and promote the child's health,
        development and welfare;

(b) the responsibility to provide the child with direction and guidance;

(c) the responsibility to maintain personal relations and direct contact with the child if the parent and child are not living together;

(d) the responsibility to act as the child's legal representative.

Section 2 of the 1995 Act sets out the parental rights that parents have in order to allow them to fulfil the responsibilities listed in s 1. These are as follows:

(a) the right to determine where the child is to reside;

(b) the right to control, direct and guide the child;

(c) the right to maintain personal relations and direct contact with the child if not living with the child;

(d) the right to act as the child's legal representative.

No responsibility or right can now be traced to the common law and parents wishing to make decisions as to the proper upbringing of the child must do so by reference to one or more of the above responsibilities or rights. Though it is usually the case that two persons will be sharing parental responsibilities and parental rights, either one may act without the consent of the other. Only one decision *always* requires the consent of both parents, and that is the removal of the child from the United Kingdom.

Responsibility (a) is the broadest of all the responsibilities and rights and will govern most decisions that a parent must make. It rests with all parents who have parental responsibilities and not just those with Right (a). While it might be expected that a decision to safeguard the child's health, development and welfare will be in its best interests, there is much scope for disagreement. If parents agree on a particular matter then their decision will govern unless it is clearly harmful to the child. If the parents disagree, it is the court that determines where the child's interests lie, by a process described in the next chapter.

Responsibility (b) needs to be read in the light of Right (b), and so the direction and guidance that the parent offers must be seen in light of the obligation to direct and guide. Responsibility (c) and Right (c) come into existence only when the parent and the child are not living together. This might be because the father has never lived with the mother, or because they previously lived together but have since separated. In either case, it is the parental responsibility, and the child's right, that family life be maintained between the absent parent and the child, at least to the extent of direct contact between the two (and it is the responsibility of the residence parent to permit and encourage this contact to take place). Responsibility (d) and Right (d) together give the parent power to act in legal transactions on behalf of the child, though this power exists only while the child does not have legal capacity to act on his or her own behalf. The child may acquire such capacity before the age of 16 (see Chapter 1 above), in which case the parent loses the power to act as legal representative. When the parent does act as legal representative he or she must make decisions on the basis of the welfare of the child but, subject to that, has the power to do whatever the child, if of full age, could have done himself or herself.

Aliment

The obligation to aliment is the obligation to provide financially for the child. This was a common law obligation and is now contained in the first seven sections of the Family Law (Scotland) Act 1985. The obligation is to provide such support as is reasonable in the circumstances for the child's upkeep and it lasts until the child is 18 years old, or 25 years old if the child over 18 is undergoing full-time education (1985 Act, s 1(5)). The obligation is normally fulfilled by the parent providing housing, food and clothing for the child, and in legal terms it goes little beyond that. Most parents, of course, expend far more than the minimum demanded by the law. A claim for aliment in a court is usually made when the family has broken up and the now absent parent is not paying what the residence parent perceives as a fair share. But it is important to note that the obligation is not to provide a fair share of the full and actual upbringing costs but merely to provide the minimum the law requires. An action for aliment is not competent in situations in which a claim for child support can be made, through the Child Support Agency and governed by the oft-amended Child Support Act 1991. This is designed to ensure a fair sharing of the real costs though the technical details are too complex to go into here. In practice, however, since child support ends at 16, actions for aliment are today limited to claims by persons over that age and are commonly raised by students seeking parental contributions to their living expenses while at college or university.

Education

Children have a right to education (Standards in Schools etc (Scotland) Act 2000) and parents have a duty to provide efficient education suitable to the child's age, ability and aptitude (Education (Scotland) Act 1980, s 30). Mostly this duty is fulfilled by sending a child to school, but the obligation is to provide education rather than to send the child to school and so if a parent can provide efficient education by other means, this is acceptable. It is an offence for the parent to fail to fulfil this duty without reasonable excuse. More recent legislation has emphasised the importance of parental choice of schools, but it has been remarkably silent on the issue of children's choice. Article 2 of Protocol 1 of the ECHR provides that no person shall be denied the right to education and that the state shall respect the right of parents to ensure such education and teaching in conformity with their own religious and philosophical convictions. So here again the issue of education is constructed around parents. Parents cannot, however, use their religious beliefs in the beating of children to insist that the state allows corporal punishment of children in schools.

Essential Facts

- Parental responsibilities and parental rights (PR & PR) attach to all mothers, and fathers who are registered as the father.
- Either parent may exercise their PR & PR independently of the other, except that the consent of both is always needed to remove the child from the UK.
- Where parents agree, their own judgement as to where the child's interests lie will normally govern; where parents disagree, it is for the court to determine the child's welfare.
- Children have a legal right to be properly educated and it is a criminal offence for parents to fail to ensure that they receive it.

Essential Cases

Gillick v West Norfolk & Wisbech Area Health Authority (1986). Mrs Gillick was the mother of 10 children and wanted to decide everything about their upbringing, including their access to sexual health care, until they were 16. She sought a guarantee from the Health Authority that they would not provide any of her children with such health care without her knowledge and consent. The Health Authority refused to give this guarantee.

The House of Lords held that children were entitled to health care without their parent's agreement if they understood the nature of the treatment and (in English law) if it was in their interests to receive it. Parents have rights, they said, only in order to allow them to fulfil their responsibilities towards their children.

Peebles v MacPhail (1990). Mrs Peebles was visiting a friend's house with her 2 year old son when he threw a tantrum. Mrs Peebles got angry and slapped the boy on the face, "with moderate force". She was charged with and convicted of assault. On appeal she claimed that the slap was reasonable chastisement and that the fact that she was angry did not convert reasonable chastisement into assault with evil intent.

The High Court upheld her conviction: "to slap a child of two on the face knocking him over was an act as remote from reasonable chastisement as it was possible to imagine".

R v Secretary of State for Education, ex parte Williamson (2005). Corporal punishment in British schools had been banned as a result of decisions of the European Court of Human Rights holding such punishment to be an infringement of, first, parents' philosophical convictions (as protected by Art 2 of Protocol 1 of the European Convention on Human Rights) not to have their children beaten and, second, of children's rights not to be subjected to inhuman or degrading treatment (as guaranteed by Art 3 of the ECHR).

Teachers and parents at four Christian schools argued that this total ban on corporal punishment was incompatible with the ECHR since it was an infringement of *their* right to freedom of religion and freedom to manifest their religious beliefs in practice by hitting children as punishment for their misdeeds.

The House of Lords held that, since non-violent means of discipline are available to teachers, a total ban on physical punishment was a proportionate balance between religious convictions and the need to protect children from undue violence.

Re J (2000). A child was born to a mixed marriage: his father was Muslim and his mother was non-Muslim. The parents separated and the child remained with the mother. The father then sought to ensure that the child was circumcised. The mother opposed this and the father raised an action to enforce his wishes.

The court held that in any situation in which the parents could not agree in respect of an issue of the upbringing of the child, the court had to determine the issue on the basis of what was in the child's best interests. In this case it was not in the child's best interests to be circumcised and so the father's action failed. Had the parents agreed, circumcision would have been lawful.

Re C (A Child) (Immunisation: Parental Rights) (2003). A mother and estranged father disagreed as to whether the child should receive the MMR triple vaccine. The mother wanted to refuse consent and argued that it was for her as the child's primary carer to decide the issue by weighing up in her own mind the risks and benefits of this procedure.

The Court of Appeal held that in cases of parental disagreement the matter did not fall to the primary carer but was rather to be resolved by the court's assessment of what was in the child's interests. The fears of autism arising from the triple vaccine were dismissed by the court as "junk science" and they held that it was clearly in the child's interests to be given the vaccine: the real risks of measles, mumps or rubella were very significantly greater than a hypothetical risk of an injury that research suggested was negligible if it existed at all.

Re A (Conjoined Twins: Medical Treatment) (2001). Siamese twins were born to a couple who held devout religious beliefs in the sanctity of life. The medical prognosis was that unless an attempt were made to separate the twins, neither would survive very long. The problem was that any attempt to save the better-developed child would most certainly kill the less-developed child. The parents were irreconcilably opposed to any procedure that would lead to the certain death of either twin. The Health Authority sought court authorisation to proceed with the separation, in the full knowledge that it would kill one twin.

The Court of Appeal held that the operation should go ahead. The best interests of the better-developed child required this and it was her only hope of life. The less-developed child would either die during the operation or die in any case, taking her sister with her, and so had no best interests to serve.

4 COURT ORDERS REGULATING THE UPBRINGING OF CHILDREN

The Court of Session and the sheriff court have the power to make orders in relation to parental responsibilities, parental rights, guardianship or the administration of a child's property (Children (Scotland) Act 1995, s 11). This will typically be when parents separate and they cannot agree on some matter such as, for example, with whom the child is to live, or how often the absent parent is to see the child, or whether the child should take a new name (such as the name of the residence parent's new partner); but an order might also be sought in a variety of other circumstances. For example, the parents may be in disagreement as to how the child is to be educated, or what medical treatment he or she is to receive, or whether the child should be allowed to accompany one parent who wishes to emigrate in pursuit of a new life, or how property that the child has acquired should be administered. Though it is normally a dispute between parents that creates a court action, this may not always be the case and the court may be asked to resolve a dispute between a parent and grandparents, or between the parents and the child's medical advisers.

The overarching principles

However a dispute arises in relation to parental responsibilities, parental rights, guardianship or the administration of a child's property, the court is bound to decide that dispute by taking account of three principles, sometimes referred to as "the overarching principles", which are contained in s 11(7) of the 1995 Act. These are as follows:

(a) The court must regard the welfare of the child as its paramount consideration. Other considerations may be relevant but the most important of all and the factor that will normally determine the case is the court's assessment of which decision will best further the child's welfare. Of course the welfare test on its own is meaningless without the court also bearing in mind a range of factors that affect (or at least are perceived to affect) the child's welfare and the court has no option but to make its own assessment of the value of a number of factors – such as the importance of a religious upbringing, the importance of maintaining a link with the child's past, the relevance of domestic violence within the household, the value of continuity of relationships and now, of course, the necessity to ensure that the family life protected by Article 8 of the European Convention is properly respected. The only matter that the court is explicitly required to have regard to in determining the child's welfare is the need to protect the child from any domestic abuse or risk of domestic abuse, either direct or indirect (ie towards the child or another family member): 1995 Act, s 11(7A)–(7E), as inserted by s 24 of the Family Law (Scotland) Act 2006.

(b)   The court is obliged to make no order unless it considers that it would be better for the child that the order be made than that none should be made at all. This is the so-called "no-order principle" under which the court must be positively persuaded that making an order will in fact further the child's best interests. This is an important brake on unnecessary orders and is a recognition that it may often be the case that the sorts of disputes that are mentioned above cannot be satisfactorily resolved by court decree. Parliament has given guidance with this principle that, wherever possible, matters should be regulated by the parties without the intervention of the courts. This principle finds reflection in the "proportionality" principle in European Human Rights law, whereby state interference in private or family life is legitimate only insofar as it is proportionate to the aim sought to be achieved.

(c)   Taking account of the child's age and maturity, the court shall so far as practicable give the child the opportunity to indicate whether he or she wishes to express any views on the matter in dispute; if the child indicates that he or she does wish to express views, give him or her the opportunity to do so; and have regard to these views. This obligation can be traced to Article 12 of the UN Convention on the Rights of the Child. It is not an obligation to give effect to the child's views and no child has the right to decide the matter before the court. Rather, it is considered proper that the court take account of such views as the child is willing to express, but always bearing in mind the court's primary obligation to decide the case, with the child's welfare being the paramount consideration. The older and more (mentally) mature the child is, the less likely it is that the court will go against his or her wishes, but that is not because the child has a right to decide but because the older the child is, the more likely it will not be in his or her welfare to be made to do something he or she does not wish to do. A child who is 12 years of age or over shall be presumed to be of sufficient maturity to form a view (1995 Act, s 11(10)), but this does not mean that children under 12 are presumed to be of insufficient maturity. Rather, each child has to be considered individually and taking account of the complexity of the issue at hand.

The available orders

The court has a variety of orders at its disposal, and they are listed in s 11(2) of the 1995 Act:

(a) An order depriving a person of some or all of his or her parental responsibilities and parental rights. Remembering the "no-order principle", this provision must be utilised if a person is to lose any aspect of their power to be involved in the bringing up of the child. Merely to stop living with the child, even when that living arrangement is sanctioned by the court, does not in itself deprive the absent parent of any parental responsibility or parental right and so he (for typically the absent parent is the father rather than the mother) is still fully entitled to be involved in the decision-making processes relating to the child's education, medical treatment, and any other aspect of upbringing. Only an order under this provision actively depriving a parent of parental responsibilities will give the residence parent the right to make decisions on her own. And, bearing in mind the "welfare principle" it will have to be shown why an order depriving an absent (or any other) parent of some aspect of parental responsibility is in the child's best interests – the court will not assume that it is best for a child that the residence parent have exclusive decision-making power. In this way the law tries to encourage both parents even after separation to remain fully involved in their children's lives – though many residence parents resent this continued involvement because it is necessarily an involvement in their own lives too.

(b) An order imposing parental responsibilities or giving parental rights. This will be appropriate when the person who is in fact caring for the child and is actively involved in the child's upbringing does not in law have any parental responsibilities and parental rights. This might be, for example, a grandparent with whom the child lives because of the parents' incapacity, absence, or death. Or it might be the residence parent's new partner (a step-parent or co-parent) who drives the child to school every day and helps with the child's homework every evening and who seeks to persuade the court that it is in the child's best interests that he be involved in schooling decisions. It should be noted that there is no limit on the number of persons who may hold at any one time parental responsibilities and parental rights and so an order granting a co-parent such responsibilities and rights does not take them away from any other person (such as the absent parent). Removal of parental responsibilities would in any case require to be sought under para (a) above.

(c) An order regulating the arrangements as to with whom, or with whom during what periods, the child is to live. This is known as a residence order and is most frequently sought on parental separation where both parents want the child to live with him or her. An order under this paragraph does no more (bearing in mind the "no-order principle") than it says. In other words, it merely regulates where the child is to live and it does not give exclusive decision-making rights, or even precedence, to the parent who is granted residence of the child (as the pre-1995 law, which used the terminology of "custody", was assumed to do). The court can make an order in a variety of different ways here, such as requiring the child to live with one parent all the time and never with the other, or with one parent during the week and the other during the weekend, or with one parent during school term-time and the other during school vacations. The court may require the child to live with someone other than parents, such as, for example, a grandparent or even an elder sibling: if it does so, then full parental responsibilities and parental rights are carried with the residence order (1995 Act, s 11(12)).

(d) An order regulating the arrangements for maintaining personal relations and direct contact between the child and a person with whom the child is not living. This is known as a contact order and will be used typically to regulate the arrangements for the non-residence parent after parental separation to see the child on a regular basis. Again, this order does no more than it says: it regulates arrangements. There is no limitation on who can benefit from a contact order and so while usually it will be designed to regulate contact between the child and an absent father, it can also regulate contact between the child and a grandparent, sibling (even if under 16), other relative or a friend or neighbour. As with a residence order, the court is given maximum flexibility to make any order that it deems to be in the interests of the child. It should be noted, however, that court orders have a tendency to freeze arrangements and an arrangement that was suitable when the parents separate may not be suitable for the child even a year or two later when he or she is older, more independent and with new friends and interests.

(e) An order regulating any specific question that has arisen. This is known as a "specific issue order" and is primarily designed to deal with one-off issues rather than the continuing issue of residence or contact. So, if there is a dispute as to the child's medical treatment, religious upbringing or name, the court may be asked to resolve the dispute (by determining what would be best for the child) under this paragraph.

(f) An interdict. This would be appropriate to prevent someone doing something, even when it is within their rights to do so, whenever the applicant can show to the satisfaction of the court that the defender's intention would be harmful to the child's interests. So, a parent may be interdicted from removing the child from the jurisdiction if this is considered dangerous, or from subjecting the child to untried and experimental medical treatment, or from being brought up within the confines of a religion whose practices are socially isolating or otherwise considered damaging.

(g) An order appointing a judicial factor. A judicial factor is a court officer who controls property on behalf of another and an order under this paragraph would be useful, therefore, whenever the child comes to own a significant amount of money which the parents for some reason (for example, due to financial inexperience) ought not to be left to look after.

(h) An order appointing or removing a person as guardian. A person can be appointed as guardian (or parent-substitute) of the child by a parent or guardian in their will to act after the death of the parent or guardian. This appointment is not limited by the "best interests test", but the court can be asked to remove such a guardian if it is not in the child's interests for guardianship under that person to continue. The court can also make an appointment of its own under this paragraph.

Title to seek an order

Any of these orders may be sought by any person who either has parental responsibilities and parental rights or who claims an interest in the child and his or her welfare. Indeed the court may make a s 11 order of its own volition and does not need to wait until it is asked (though there needs to be some issue before the civil court in any case during which the court comes to believe that an order would further the child's welfare). The child too, himself or herself, can make an application for a s 11 order: children have capacity to sue in the civil courts whenever they have a general understanding of what it means to do so (Age of Legal Capacity (Scotland) Act 1991, s 2(4A)). So a child may seek an order removing a parent from decision-making powers, or an order requiring or allowing him or her to live with one of the parents or even someone else entirely.

There are some people who cannot seek a s 11 order. First, and more simply, are local authorities. Their powers to become involved in the upbringing of children are extensive but highly constrained and are contained in very detailed provisions in the public law sections in Part 2 of the Children (Scotland) Act 1995. Local authorities cannot avoid these detailed provisions by seeking an order under the much more straightforward s 11 (which is in the private law Part 1 of the 1995 Act). Second, any person who used to have parental responsibilities and parental rights but from whom such responsibilities and rights were removed (either by the adoption process under the Adoption (Scotland) Act 1978 or by the public law process in later provisions of the Children (Scotland) Act 1995) cannot seek to have them restored by the straightforward provisions in s 11. This exclusion from s 11 does not apply to individuals whose responsibilities and rights were earlier removed by an order under s 11 itself.

Essential Facts

- All disputes between individuals in relation to the upbringing of children are to be resolved with the child's welfare being the paramount consideration.

- The child must always be given an opportunity to express views on the dispute and the court must not make any order unless it considers that it would be better for the child to do so than not to do so.
- A parent's PR & PR continue after parental separation.
- A child just as much as a parent has title to seek a s 11 order to regulate any aspect of his or her upbringing.
- A parent whose PR & PR have been removed by an adoption order or other public law process cannot seek their restoration by means of a s 11 order.

Essential Cases

Brixey v Lynas (1996). Emma Brixey was a single teenage mother when she met the schoolboy Michael Lynas who was attending a boarding school close to where she lived and worked. They started having sex, Emma became pregnant again and a little girl was born when Emma was 20 and Michael was 18. After living for a short period of time together with Michael's parents, the relationship broke down and Emma returned north. Michael then raised an action for custody of the little girl, and the sheriff granted him custody on the basis that Mrs Lynas (Michael's mother and the child's grandmother) would be able to look after the girl better than the flighty, immature Emma. The Inner House overruled this on the ground that the sheriff had failed to take account of the need of a young child for its mother. Michael appealed to the House of Lords on the basis that the Inner House had placed too much emphasis on a "maternal preference".

The House of Lords held that while there is no rule of law or principle or presumption that very young children should remain with their mothers, it was nevertheless a fact of nature which had to be taken into account that a very young child's need for his or her mother is usually greater than his or her need for the father. The child stayed with her mother.

Osborne v Matthan (No 2) (1998). Althea Matthan was a native of Jamaica. She came to the United Kingdom where she supported herself and her young daughter, Fiona, through prostitution and drug-dealing. When Fiona was 2, Althea was imprisoned in

England. Althea asked her neighbour and (then) friend Mrs Helen Osborne to look after Fiona. Three years later, when Althea was about to be released from jail, it became apparent that on her release she would be deported back to Jamaica. At this stage Mrs Osborne moved to Perth and she sought a residence order to retain Fiona and to prevent her being returned to her mother, and returned to Jamaica. The sheriff awarded residence to Mrs Osborne and Althea appealed against that decision.

The Inner House held that the decision had to stand. Though mothers have primary rights in disputes with strangers the fundamental issue is always what is in the best interests of the child and here it was clear that Mrs Osborne could give Fiona a much better upbringing than the indigent and homeless Ms Matthan who was on the brink of being deported to a poverty-struck country.

Porchetta v Porchetta (1986). Mr and Mrs Porchetta divorced when their child was very young. Mrs Porchetta was awarded what was then called custody of the child and Mr Porchetta sought access to his child. Mrs Porchetta was hostile to her ex-husband and his presence was causing her, and consequently the child, distress: she refused to allow him to see the child.

Mr Porchetta went to court for an access order on the basis that he was entitled to access with his own child. The court held that so-called parental "rights" are not rights in the sense of being automatically enforceable, and that he had to prove that it would be in the welfare of the child to grant the order sought.

Early v Early (1990). Mr and Mrs Early separated and the youngest child remained with Mrs Early, the two older children going with Mr Early. He subsequently picked up two convictions for child neglect. Mrs Early, however, did something much worse: she entered into a lesbian relationship. Shocked, and thinking only of his poor boy-child, Mr Early sought custody of the youngest child (by now 7 years of age).

The court removed the little boy from the mother with whom he had always lived, on the basis that the father (notwithstanding his convictions for child neglect) would provide him with a male role model and he might otherwise suffer teasing at school. It didn't work, of course.

White v White (2001). Mr and Mrs White separated, the two children remaining with Mrs White. Mr White had generous contact with his daughters, until he entered into a relationship with a new woman. The new woman fell out with Mrs White. Mrs White refused thereafter to allow Mr White contact with the girls. He raised an action seeking a contact order. At first instance, the sheriff held that since the Children (Scotland) Act 1995 assumed that contact with both parents should continue, that should be his starting point. In other words, the onus was on Mrs White to show why contact should be stopped. On appeal the sheriff principal disagreed and held that the "no-order principle" or "minimum intervention principle" in the 1995 Act placed the onus on the person seeking the order (Mr White) to show that it would be beneficial to make the order. Mr White appealed to the Court of Session.

That court held that there was no onus one way or the other. The court had to weigh up whether it was or was not in the interests of the child to have the order made. The so-called "minimum intervention principle" was simply an indication that Parliament believed that it was better that children did not have unnecessary orders over them.

X v Y (2002). A lesbian couple persuaded a gay male friend to provide some sperm with which one of them could become pregnant. When the child was born the father (as he saw himself) and sperm-donor (as the women regarded him) was allowed regular contact until the child was around 6 weeks old at which point the women refused to allow him any further part in the child's life. He sought a contact order under s 11 of the Children (Scotland) Act 1995. The partner of the mother counter-claimed with her own action to seek a residence order, shared with the mother.

The sheriff held that it was in the interests of the child to have some contact with the father and so made the contact order in his favour. But she refused to make a residence order in favour of the co-parent, on the basis that there was no "family". (The Act does not require any "family" relationship to exist before an order is made and in any case after *Fitzpatrick v Sterling Housing Association* (see Chapter 7) a same-sex couple can be regarded as "family": the sheriff's reasoning is flawed here).

D v H (2004). D, a 15 year old boy, sought a contact order in terms of the Children (Scotland) Act 1995, s 11(2)(d) so that he could have contact with X, his blood-sister who had been adopted by H some years previously. The sheriff held that since contact is a "parental responsibility and parental right" which could be imposed only on adults, he had no title.

This decision is wrong (and has not been followed in other sheriff court cases). A contact order can regulate contact between the child and any other person, not just between the child and the child's parents.

Sanderson v McManus (1997). Stuart Sanderson raised an action against Jane McManus for paternity and access over a little boy, Bradley. Jane did not dispute Stuart's paternity claim but she resisted allowing him any access to their son. Interim access was permitted before the case went to proof but during that time the boy, then aged 4, alleged that his father had hit him and at the proof further access was denied. The case went to the House of Lords.

The court held that while the boy's evidence could not be taken as proof of what he said (because of his age), the boy's behaviour was a matter to be taken into account. The father's claim for access had to be based on more than the fact that he was the father: the question was always whether contact was likely to benefit the child and the sheriff's decision that there was no benefit could not be criticised by an appeal court. So the father lost access.

Shields v Shields (2002). When Mrs Claire Shields and Mr Nicholas Shields separated, it was agreed informally that the child, D, would remain with Mrs Shields but that Mr Shields would have regular contact with his son. When the child was 7, Mrs Shields was offered a career opportunity in Australia, which she wished to take, but Mr Shields refused to consent to D being removed from the United Kingdom. Mrs Shields sought a specific issue order under s 11(2)(e) of the Children (Scotland) Act 1995, allowing her to take her son to Australia without the father's consent. The sheriff granted her this order, and the sheriff principal upheld his decision. Mr Shields appealed to the Court of Session.

That court held that the "overarching principles" in the Children (Scotland) Act 1995 required that the decision be made on the basis of what was best for the child. Was it better for D to move with his mother where she would have better career opportunities, or to remain in Scotland where his relationship with his father could continue and develop? The decision also required that D be given the opportunity to express views. Neither the sheriff nor the sheriff principal had given D the opportunity to express views and so their decision could not stand. (The child then expressed the view that he did not wish to relocate to Australia and so the order sought by the mother was denied.)

5 STATE INTERFERENCE IN THE UPBRINGING OF CHILDREN

As we have seen, although Scots law, by and large, allows parents and others with parental responsibilities and parental rights to determine how their children are to be brought up, there are various obligations imposed on parents and various expectations as to how they will fulfil their duties. Similarly, although Scots law is obliged by Article 8 of the European Convention on Human Rights to respect the right to family life inhering in both parent and child, the state is also obliged to ensure that children are not subjected to abuse, neglect, torture and inhuman or degrading treatment. Since the horrid truth is that far more children suffer in this way at the hands of their own parents than at the hands of strangers, it follows that, in order to fulfil its duty towards children, the state is sometimes obliged to act against the parents and to require that children are subjected to care and protection measures against the wishes of their own parents. The power of the state to do so is contained in a number of provisions, the most important of which is Part 2 of the Children (Scotland) Act 1995. But other Acts to take note of are the Children and Young Persons (Scotland) Act 1937, which makes it an offence to neglect a child to such an extent that he or she is likely to suffer significant harm; the Matrimonial Homes (Family Protection) (Scotland) Act 1981, which allows for the granting of matrimonial and other interdicts against the owner or occupier of a property in which the child lives when this is necessary for the safety of the child; the Protection from Abuse (Scotland) Act 2001, which allows the court to attach powers of arrest to interdicts (that is to say, allows the police to become involved in the enforcement of the civil remedy of interdict); the Protection of Children (Scotland) Act 2003, which obliges organisations who deal with children to carry out police checks on those employed by the organisations; and the Anti-Social Behaviour etc (Scotland) Act 2004, which permits the courts to make "parenting orders" over parents whose upbringing skills are wanting. The most important mechanism for protecting children is the children's hearing system.

The children's hearing system

Background and philosophy

The children's hearing system is uniquely Scottish. It was established by the Social Work (Scotland) Act 1968 and underwent significant modification in Part 2 of the Children (Scotland) Act 1995, though the underlying philosophy of the system was maintained in 1995. The system represents a deliberate attempt to get away from formalised court-based systems for dealing with both juvenile offenders and children who were abused and neglected and it was avowedly welfarist in its outlook. And so it remains.

There are a number of underlying philosophies within the system. First, it is assumed that children who have committed a criminal offence (the so-called "juvenile offender") ought to be treated in the same process as children who are being abused or neglected. The reason for this is that in both situations the system aims to get to the underlying problem facing the child rather than to respond to the events that have brought the child to the attention of the authorities. And it is a truth that is often denied, but remains the truth nevertheless, that the underlying problems are the same for both categories of children. These problems – parental unemployment, low educational achievements, drug and alcohol abuse, domestic violence, social exclusion – may be manifested through different children in different ways, but they are in essence the same. Second, the system proceeds on the basis that a formal court setting and process may well be ideal to determine the facts upon which the child is brought within the system, but is far from ideal in determining the appropriate response to the various problems facing the child and his or her family. So while disputes of fact may be resolved in a court of law, determining the disposal is in the sole remit of a panel of trained but essentially lay persons – the children's hearing. Being drawn from a much wider section of the community than any bench of judges, or even sheriffs, the children's hearing can more readily be trusted to determine whether any particular style of upbringing of a child is simply not acceptable to general Scottish society today. And third, the system is almost exclusively welfare-based. In other words, the outcome in any particular case is determined by the children's hearing making its decisions on the basis of the welfare of the child. The hearing is *not* aiming to "punish" either the child or the parent or to make an order appropriate to the child's "offence" or the parent's "badness". The aim is to see what is the best way forward for the child after it has been established that the upbringing of the child is, in some way, presently failing. And fourth, following on from this, the hearing system is designed to take a holistic view of the child and his or her whole environment. This is only proper since in the vast majority of cases to come before a children's hearing it is the family background to which the child's difficulties can be traced.

The process

The key figure in the process is an individual known as the children's reporter, or the reporter to the children's hearing. The first duty of the reporter is to receive information concerning the wellbeing of particular children. This information may come from a variety of sources, but will usually be from the police, schools or social services. It may come in addition from medical personnel, neighbours, friends, other family members and even (though this is virtually unknown) from the child himself or herself. The reporter must investigate the information he or she receives, and can ask for a report on the child from the social services and education departments of the local authority or the police. He or she must then make a decision as to (i) whether one of the "grounds of referral" is made out and (ii) whether, if so, compulsory measures of supervision might be required. Neither decision is conclusively for the reporter to make but it is only if he or she is of the opinion that one or more grounds are made out and that compulsory measures would benefit the child, that he or she can move on to the next stage, which is arranging a children's hearing.

At the children's hearing, which is made up of three members of the children's panel, the chairman of the hearing will ask the child and the "relevant person" (ie parent or carer of the child) whether or not they accept the accuracy of the grounds of referral. "Grounds of referral" include that the child has been abused or neglected, has committed a criminal offence, has not been attending school, or is beyond parental control (the full list of grounds is found in s 52(2) of the Children (Scotland) Act 1995). If either does not accept the accuracy of the stated ground, or the child is too young to understand, the hearing has the choice of either discharging the referral or sending the matter to the sheriff court for proof – disputes as to the facts upon which the grounds of referral are based are matters for the sheriff and not for the hearing to resolve. But if the sheriff resolves the dispute by finding grounds established, the hearing will reconvene and must accept the facts as found by the sheriff. If the sheriff finds the grounds not established, the referral is discharged.

The purpose of the hearing is to discuss with the child and the relevant persons the grounds of referral and any other background information that might help the hearing to determine what the outcome should be. The aim is to find a solution that is in the best interests of the child and will resolve the problem that brought the child to the hearing. If the hearing does not discharge the referral it will impose a supervision requirement on the child, but that may be subject to such terms and conditions as the hearing thinks fit, and these terms and conditions clearly will differ depending upon the child's needs. It may be, in a care and protection case, that all the child needs is for his or her upbringing to be supervised by social workers, or that the child needs to be removed temporarily from dangerous and dirty home conditions. Rarely, the child may need to be removed with little expectation that he or she will return – but this would be an appropriate outcome only in the most extreme of circumstances when there is virtually no chance of the parents being able to change their styles of life sufficiently to provide the child with the minimum standard of care. In a case where the child has committed an offence it may be that the terms of the supervision requirement oblige the child to attend group work to address offending behaviour, or (though this is rare) to meet his or her victim and to make practical reparation. Whatever the ground of referral, and not just in cases involving offences, the child may be required to reside at a children's home and it is possible to attach a condition that the child be locked up. Such an extreme outcome should never be seen in terms of "punishment", for that is not the purpose of the children's hearing system. But a child who is in trouble may well need the stability and control of secure accommodation before any work in addressing his or her life problems can begin.

There is of course an appeal procedure from decisions of the children's hearing, to the sheriff then the sheriff principal and then (or directly from the sheriff) the Court of Session (but not thereafter to the House of Lords). And any supervision requirement that has been imposed upon the child must be reviewed within a year, or earlier if requested by the local authority, the child or relevant person, or the hearing that originally imposed it. In any case, if not brought to an end at a review before then, the supervision requirement will terminate on the child's 18th birthday.

Emergency protection

It sometimes happens that a local authority are of the view that a child needs to be removed from his or her home environment even before a children's hearing has had a chance to consider the case fully and properly. This will be the case whenever it is of the view that the child is at risk of serious harm unless action is taken immediately. In these circumstances the local authority can apply to the sheriff for a "child protection order" (s 68 of the 1995 Act) which, if granted, lasts a maximum of 8 working days. During that time, while the child is kept away from his or her family, the reporter will draw up grounds of referral and the hearing that has to be held on the 8th working day after the removal of the child will consider the child's case. If, during the process and before a decision can be made, the child continues to require to be kept away from home this may be done by means of a warrant granted by the hearing.

Police officers also have the power to remove a child summarily from a source of imminent danger but their power lasts for only 24 hours: during this time the local authority will be contacted and it is for them to decide whether to seek a child protection order (and thereafter for the reporter to decide whether to arrange a children's hearing).

Child protection and the European Convention

Removing a child from its parents, or even interfering in the upbringing of a child by means of a supervision requirement under which the child remains at home, is, necessarily, an interference with both the child's and the parents' right to private and family life, respect for which is guaranteed by Article 8(1) of the European Convention on Human Rights. It follows that such interference must be justified by Article 8(2), that is to say must be "necessary in a democratic society". What this means is that the aim of the interference must be in accordance with the law, follow a legitimate aim (which is easy to establish since protection of children is not only legitimate but a state obligation) and be "proportionate" to that aim, or no more severe than is necessary to achieve that aim. The proportionality test finds reflection in s 16 of the 1995 Act, under which the hearing and the court must make decisions for the welfare of the child that are the minimum necessary. It has been held on numerous occasions by the European Court of Human Rights that any decision to have a child permanently removed from his or her parents can be justified only in the most extreme of circumstances, and that the aim of state intervention must always have as its ultimate goal family reunification. But that Court does recognise that in some cases this will simply not be possible and that a child's interests may very occasionally require a complete cessation of family life with his or her existing family.

Essential Facts

- The children's hearing system is based on a philosophy that children who offend are as much in need of care and protection as children who have been offended against.
- The children's hearing determines what is in the interests of the child, but the court determines whether a ground of referral exists or not (if the matter is disputed or the child is too young to accept the ground).
- Once the grounds of referral have been established, the hearing may take into account any other facts that are relevant to the child's welfare.
- A child protection order may be granted by a sheriff to provide immediate protection to a child in an emergency: this will permit the summary removal of the child and the keeping of the child in a place of safety for 8 working days.
- Removal of a child from his or her home is an infringement of Article 8(1) of the European Convention on Human Rights, and it therefore requires justification under Article 8(2) as being a proportionate response to the danger facing the child.
- The ultimate aim of all child care proceedings should be to return the child to his or her family.

Essential Cases

Sloan v B (1991). Nine children from four families in Orkney were removed from their parents after allegations of ritualistic and sadistic abuse. They were referred to a children's hearing, which dispensed with their presence. The parents denied the grounds of referral and the sheriff dismissed the grounds on the basis of procedural irregularity, being that the children had been excluded from their own hearing on the basis that they would not understand, before the hearing had carried out any assessment of their understanding. The children were returned home.

On appeal, the Inner House held that the sheriff had been wrong to dismiss the grounds on procedural arguments: he ought to have heard the evidence first. The fact that the children were wrongly excluded from their own hearing was a "mere technicality". But the case was not proceeded with and the children remained with their parents.

O v Rae (1993). Four children were referred to a children's hearing on the basis of lack of parental care, and supervision requirements were made over the four children, requiring them to live in residential accommodation away from their father. At a review of this requirement the social background report referred to an allegation that the father had sexually abused the eldest child and the hearing decided to continue the supervision requirement. The father appealed on the ground that the allegation had never been tested in evidence and so it ought not to have been allowed to influence the decision of the hearing.

The Court of Session held that the hearing had been correct to take into account allegations made in a social background report, even when these facts were denied and had not been tested in evidence. All that is required to be proved in evidence is facts making up the grounds of referral, and the outcome of any case can be determined by other facts since the hearing is able to look at all the circumstances of the case, including those circumstances denied by one or more of the parties.

S v Miller (2001). A child was referred to the children's hearing on account of his involvement in a violent incident with numerous individuals, which led to the death of his father. The hearing authorised his detention in secure accommodation. The child challenged the procedure as being contrary to Article 6 of the European Convention on Human Rights since he had not been allowed paid legal representation at the hearing.

The court held that a blanket ban on legal aid for representation of children at hearings was not compatible with the ECHR.

P v P (2000). Where would the child protection system be without grandparents? A child was made subject to a supervision requirement by a children's hearing under Part 2 of the Children (Scotland) Act 1995, requiring him to reside with his maternal grandmother. The grandmother then sought a residence order under Part 1 of the 1995 Act. The mother did not oppose the action, but the father did. He counter-claimed and sought parental responsibilities over the child. The sheriff held that during the currency of the supervision requirement neither the grandmother nor the father could seek an order under Part 1 of the Act since this might conflict with the conditions in the requirement made under Part 2 of the Act.

The grandmother appealed and the Court of Session held that Parts 1 and 2 of the 1995 Act were not entirely separate and distinct schemes but were both designed to advance the child's welfare. Nothing in Part 2 made an order under Part 1 incompetent, though any parental responsibility or right governed by Part 1 could not be exercised in a way that was inconsistent with a supervision requirement made under Part 2. So the order could be sought, but if granted its exercise would be constrained by the terms of the supervision requirement.

Johansen v Norway (1997). A baby was removed from her mother on birth and placed with foster carers. The mother was inadequate, did not look after herself or her children, was addicted to anti-depressants, was starving herself and had been in a series of violent relationships; she was mentally unstable.

The European Court held that the decision to remove the baby was not contrary to Article 8 of the ECHR, but that the decision by the authorities to prevent any access between mother and child was a breach. Removal was a proportionate response to the difficulties but refusing access made it increasingly difficult to aim for the reintegration of the child with the mother, which should be the ultimate aim of all child protection processes.

Scott v United Kingdom (2000). An alcoholic woman gave birth to a baby girl who was suffering from fetal alcohol syndrome. After treatment, the baby was allowed to be removed by the mother. The mother's alcohol abuse continued and she was unable to care for the child properly so the father (who was not married to the mother) took the child to the social services department of the local authority and left her there. The local authority placed the child with foster carers and sought to help the mother address her alcohol problems. After 2½ years it was obvious that no progress was being made and the local authority then sought to free the child for adoption. The mother refused to agree but the court dispensed with her consent to adoption. She then took the British government to the European Court of Human Rights on the basis that her right to family life under Article 8 had been infringed by the dispensing with her agreement.

The European Court held that the decision-making process in this case had not denied the mother opportunities to participate, that there was no chance of her resuming care of her child while her alcoholism persisted, that there was no foreseeable chance of her being cured of alcoholism, and that therefore although the decision of the domestic courts meant that her family life with her child would be terminated, this was a proportionate response to the problem. So there was no breach of Article 8.

6 MARRIAGE AND CIVIL PARTNERSHIP

The conjugal relationships that adults enter into are governed by the law on two different levels, depending upon the formality of the relationship. By "conjugal relationships" is meant here domestic relationships entered into voluntarily by "couples" combining their social, emotional and financial lives together. They are relationships which start out as, or develop into (but do not necessarily remain) sexual. Though not entirely accurate (as we will see) it is convenient to classify conjugal relationships as those which are registered with the state (as either marriage or civil partnership) and those which are not so registered. Marriage is the registered relationship of opposite-sex couples; civil partnership is the registered relationship of same-sex couples. Unregistered relationships ("cohabiting couples") are examined in the next chapter.

Entering into registered relationships

The statutory means of entering into both marriages and civil partnerships are largely but not completely the same: they are set out in the Marriage (Scotland) Act 1977 and the Civil Partnership Act 2004. The parties must give notice to the district registrar of their intention to marry or enter into a civil partnership, and so long as he or she is satisfied of their capacity or eligibility to do so the district registrar will issue a schedule which gives permission to proceed. In religious marriages certain church functionaries have the power to conduct the ceremony on behalf of the state; with civil marriages and civil partnerships the ceremony is conducted and controlled by the registrar. In either case the ceremony must be witnessed by two witnesses professing to be (in the case of marriage) and actually being (in the case of civil partnership) over 16 years of age; the parties must agree to be the other's husband, wife or civil partner; and after the ceremony the schedule must be registered with the district registrar. It is left largely to the parties, in negotiation with the celebrant (the church functionary or the district registrar) what form the ceremony itself is to take, but there are some limitations on where it may take place.

For marriage (though not for civil partnerships) the common law permitted parties to enter into this legal institution even without any formal ceremony and without, therefore, registration of the entering into the relationship. Of the three informal methods permitted by the common law, only one survived the statutory modernisation of Scottish marriage law in the Marriage (Scotland) Act 1939, and that remaining method will be slowly phased out from 2006. This informal method of getting married is known as marriage by cohabitation with habit and repute. The cohabitation must be for a significant length of time (so long as at least some of it takes place before the commencement of the abolishing Family Law (Scotland) Act 2006). The court has accepted periods of just short of a year. The cohabitation must have taken place at a time when the parties were, in law, free to marry each other. The "habit and repute", ie the understanding of outsiders that the couple are married, must be general and widely held but the doctrine is not avoided by showing that a small number of people knew the truth. So a couple whom most of their friends and neighbours thought were married but whose parents, say, knew had never gone through a ceremony of marriage, might well be considered to be married by the law. To establish marriage by this means it is necessary to raise an action for declarator of marriage. This by-product of an earlier age has long outlived its usefulness and was latterly simply a means by which cohabitants could gain legal rights on death or separation otherwise denied them (by pretending to be married and accessing thereby the benefits of marriage). The typical case was when one cohabitant died and the other was told she had no right to succeed to any part of the deceased's estate. There was, of course, no registration of this form of marriage, though the court decree will be proof positive whenever it is needed.

As a common law doctrine, designed to provide a route for entry into the common law institution of marriage, there was no equivalent for civil partnership which is a statutory creation.

Consequences of marriage and civil partnership

Marriage and civil partnership create a status, by which is meant that they attract rights and obligations irrespective of the factual state of the relationship, and not only between the parties *inter se* but also between each individual party and the rest of the world. The major consequences in law are as follows.

(a) Aliment

Each partner to a marriage or civil partnership is obliged to aliment the other. By this is meant that each partner must provide for the financial support of the other and, if that support is not forthcoming, each may sue the other. The rules of aliment are contained in the first seven sections of the Family Law (Scotland) Act 1985. Aliment is a statutory obligation based upon the status of marriage or civil partnership and it follows that the right to aliment terminates as soon as the marriage or civil partnership comes to an end whether on death or on divorce (though in either case the claimant may seek a part of the other's property).

(b) Succession

Spouses and civil partners cannot be disinherited. This has for long been the common law rule with spouses, and it is statutorily so for civil partners. The primary entitlement is known as legal rights, whereby the spouse or civil partner is entitled to one third of their deceased partner's moveable estate (if the partner is also survived by issue, that is to say children or grandchildren or great grandchildren etc) or one half of the moveable estate (if the deceased is not survived by any children etc). This entitlement is not in addition to any legacy that the deceased may have left his or her partner and so if there is a legacy in a will the survivor must choose to accept either the legacy or their legal rights. Another entitlement, this time statutory for both spouses and civil partners, is known as prior rights. These are paid only when the deceased dies intestate or partially intestate (ie without an effectual will). There are rights to cash, to the family home, and to the furnishings and plenishings of the family home (in each case up to stated financial limits). The rules for both spouses and civil partners are contained in ss 8 and 9 of the Succession (Scotland) Act 1964. Finally, if the deceased's estate has anything left over after the payment of legal rights and prior rights, the spouse or civil partner has a claim to the free estate that is not otherwise distributed according to a will (because either the deceased did not make a will or the will was not valid or the will did not cover all the property owned by the deceased). This right to the free estate is, however, postponed to the preferred free estate claims of the deceased's descendants, parents and siblings. Of course, it is open to a partner in a registered relationship to make a will leaving all their property to their partner (though if they do so but also leave issue, the partner takes only after payment of the legal rights claimed by such issue).

(c) Right to occupy the family home

One of the most important rights that is granted to all spouses and civil partners is the right to occupy the family home even when that home is owned exclusively by one only. This right was conferred by the Matrimonial Homes (Family Protection) (Scotland) Act 1981 and replicated for civil partners by the Civil Partnership Act 2004. It was previously relatively common for the family home to be owned only by one party – usually the husband – and in that situation before the 1981 Act the wife had neither legal title to the house nor legal right to live there: she lived in the family home on the husband's sufferance. Of course, she had a remedy of divorce if the husband excluded her but she remained homeless in these circumstances. So the 1981 Act conferred on what is called the "non-entitled spouse" (and, since the Civil Partnership Act 2004, "non-entitled partner") the right to occupy the family home. This right is good against third parties, so that it cannot be defeated by the owner of the house selling it on. The right lasts as long as the marriage or civil partnership lasts, so that at its termination (whether on death, divorce or dissolution) the right comes to an end. But death brings succession rights and divorce or dissolution brings rights to claim financial provision. If both the spouses or both the civil partners have joint title to the family home (as is much more common today) then property law rather than the 1981 Act gives both the right to occupy in any case.

(d) Protection from domestic violence

The rules here are mostly contained in the Matrimonial Homes (Family Protection) (Scotland) Act 1981, and replicated in the Civil Partnership Act 2004. These Acts provide that a spouse or civil partner can seek an exclusion order excluding their partner from the family home if this is necessary to protect themselves or any child of the family from any conduct or threatened or reasonably apprehended conduct of the other partner. On the same test a spouse or civil partner can seek an interdict against the partner. It used to be more significant that the interdict was granted under the 1981 Act since attached thereto could be a power of arrest, authorising the police to arrest a partner who breached the interdict – a power not otherwise attachable to interdicts which were seen very much as civil law remedies. Now, however, the Protection from Abuse (Scotland) Act 2001 allows the court to attach a power of arrest to any interdict designed to protect against personal violence and so the availability of an interdict under the 1981 Act or the 2004 Act is far less important today.

(e) Tax

There are various tax consequences of a person acquiring the status of married person or civil partner. This book is not the place to explore all the taxation statutes, but the most important consequence may usefully be mentioned here. This relates to Inheritance Tax. Under the Inheritance Tax Act 1984, as amended, if a person dies owning property above a certain value, the transfer of that property to his or her successors will generate a liability to taxation. Importantly, however, transfers to spouses or civil partners are exempt from this tax. The state takes the view that if property passes on the death of one partner to the other there is little lost to the public purse since on the death of the other their (now joint) estates will attract the tax liability; conversely it would be inequitable for a spouse or civil partner who inherits the estate of their deceased partner to be forced to sell part of that estate in order to pay the taxation due. That would typically be the most valuable part of the estate, the house, which would result in the survivor losing his or her home. Thus the exemption.

(f) Debts and bankruptcy

If one spouse or civil partner becomes bankrupt, the creditors are entitled to challenge any transfers the bankrupt person made to their domestic partner in the past 5 years (Bankruptcy (Scotland) Act 1985). If the family home is threatened with sale by the creditors, the non-entitled spouse or civil partner must be kept informed. Any domestic partner who has acted as the other's cautioner (guarantor for debts) can escape that obligation by showing that undue pressure was brought on them to act as such: if the creditor is aware of the relationship they are put on notice to ensure that undue pressure was not in fact brought to bear.

(g) Relationships with children

The fact that the parents of children are not and never have been married to each other used to have devastating consequences for the child. This was the old concept of "illegitimacy". Today, the effects in law of "illegitimacy" are limited to entitlement to succeed to titles of honour (like dukedoms, baronetcies, coats of arms, and the Crown). But there remain some crucial differences in terms of the legal responsibilities and legal rights that fathers have. For one thing, marriage creates a presumption of paternity. In other words, if a child is born to a married woman, her husband is presumed to be the father of the child. Another consequence of marriage is that a joint petition for adoption may be made by the couple: unmarried couples are not in Scots law permitted to adopt a child jointly (though they will be after the Adoption and Children (Scotland) Bill 2006). Similarly, only a married couple can seek a "parental order" under the Human Fertilisation and Embryology Act 1990 which will deem them parents of a child born as a result of a surrogacy arrangement. None of these consequences has been extended (in Scotland) to civil partners. While it is understandable that a presumption of paternity is not applied to the female civil partner of a woman, it is not understandable, if the aim of adoption law is to provide a stable family unit for a child, why joint adoption is not possible for same-sex couples who have committed themselves to the stabilising institution of çivil partnership. Legislation is likely to resolve this anomaly soon.

(h) Criminal law

The criminal law is affected in a number of ways by the fact that parties have married or entered into a civil partnership. First and (perhaps) most obviously, if a married or civilly enpartnered individual goes through a form of marriage or civil partnership before the end of the existing legal relationship then the new marriage or civil partnership has no effect in law. If it is a marriage, the already married party will be guilty of the crime of bigamy. This crime was originally designed to protect parties from fraudulent marriages, but the rule is probably today better understood as designed to avoid frauds on the public register since marriage and civil partnership results in the conferral of a variety of civic benefits on the parties thereto. Another consequence in the criminal law relates to the law of incest and related offences, which is governed by the Criminal Law (Consolidation) (Scotland) Act 1995. It is the crime of incest to have sexual intercourse with various members of one's genetic family. The so-called "related offences" make it a similar offence to have sexual intercourse with some of the relations of one's spouse or civil partner. So not only is it a crime to have sexual intercourse with one's own child but it is also a crime to have sexual intercourse with one's step-child (ie the child of one's spouse or civil partner): it is not automatically a crime to have sexual intercourse with one's unregistered partner's child. "Child" in all of this refers to relationship rather than age. A final consequence in the criminal law of marriage (but not of civil partnership since this common law rule was not, for good reason, extended in the statute that created civil partnership) is that a wife (and the law is entirely and deliberately gendered here) cannot be charged with resetting the goods stolen by her husband, on the ground that she has a matrimonial duty to obey him even in his criminal endeavours. A similar rule, "justified" by the same outmoded conception of the relationship of husband and wife, applies to harbouring criminals: a wife cannot be charged with the crime of harbouring a fugitive from justice if the fugitive is her husband. The contemporary social utility of this rule continues to escape great minds.

(i) Miscellaneous effects

Marriage and civil partnership has a number of other effects in law. The most important of these are, first, the rule in s 25 of the Family Law (Scotland) Act 1985 that in a question as to the ownership of any household goods (as defined in s 25(3)) it is presumed (rebuttably) that the goods are owned in common; second, the rule in s 26 of the 1985 Act that any savings from a housekeeping allowance that one makes to the other are jointly owned; third, nationality and immigration; fourth, that spouses and civil partners are entitled to refuse to give evidence that will incriminate their partner who is the accused in a criminal court case; and fifth, on the negligently caused death of one of the spouses or civil partners the other is entitled to damages under the Damages (Scotland) Act 1976 (as amended) for their loss of support and for a non-patrimonial amount designed to reflect the distress and anxiety endured by the survivor in contemplation of the suffering of the deceased, grief and sorrow, and any non-patrimonial benefit of the deceased's society and guidance, now lost.

Essential Facts

- Marriage is for opposite-sex couples and civil partnership is for same-sex couples.
- Marriage by cohabitation with habit and repute requires that at least some cohabitation between the parties occurs before the Family Law (Scotland) Act 2006 came into force.
- Marriages and civil partnerships must be celebrated and registered in the presence of both parties and two witnesses, and both parties must give free consent.
- The major consequences of marriage are alimentary obligations, succession rights, occupancy rights in the family home, extra protection from domestic violence and exemption from inheritance tax.

Essential Cases

Hyde v Hyde (1866). Hyde was an Englishman who travelled extensively in North America. He married his wife in the territory of Utah, before that part of North America entered the United States of America. It was assumed that Utah law permitted polygamy, as the Mormon faith then did (and the Fundamentalist schismatics still do): Hyde married his wife according to the rituals of the Mormons. He subsequently left both the Mormon faith and his wife, and she took another husband, a course of action allowed by her faith. Hyde, by now back in England, sought to bring his marriage to an end by divorce, on the basis of his wife's adultery. The judge, Lord Penzance, refused to grant the divorce, on the basis that there was no marriage as English law understood the concept and as such nothing to bring to an end.

Lord Penzance laid down what has come to be regarded as the common law definition of marriage: "Marriage is the voluntary union for life of one man and one woman to the exclusion of all others." He spoke at a time less than 10 years after the introduction of judicial divorce into England (though Scotland has had divorce since the Reformation).

Wetherhill v Sheikh (2005). Karen Wetherhill fell in love with Zahid Sheikh, even although he was already married to someone else. But that was an arranged marriage to which Zahid was not committed, and so Karen and Zahid moved in together, started a business together, and had two children together. Zahid's parents, with whom his (proper) wife lived, would accept Karen as a member of the family only if she were married to Zahid, so they told his parents that they were indeed married. The (proper) wife left Scotland and soon thereafter divorced Zahid. Karen was now free to marry the father of her children, but she refused to do so, fearing enveilment. Zahid's family continued to believe they were already married in any case. The relationship broke down some years later and Karen sought a declarator that they were married by cohabitation with habit and repute so that she could get financial provision on divorce.

The court held that they were married. They had lived together for 12 years and Lord Philip found that there was sufficient habit and repute. This case may have been the nail in the coffin that finally persuaded our law-makers to do away with the doctrine of marriage by cohabitation with habit and repute.

Saleh v Saleh (1987). Carol Mackie agreed to marry Abdallah Saleh and they submitted a marriage notice in Grangemouth where it was put on public display. In fact, however, the marriage took place in Edinburgh (at that city's Mosque) where there had been no notice. The relationship broke down and Carol sought a declarator of nullity. The Lord Advocate argued that under the terms of s 23A of the Marriage (Scotland) Act 1977 errors such as to the place of the ceremony could be ignored. However, no marriage schedule had been drawn up to authorise the Mosque officials to conduct a lawful marriage and the marriage was never registered. The court agreed with the Lord Advocate that these latter flaws could not be put right by s 23A.

Smith v Bank of Scotland (1997). Mrs Smith was persuaded by her husband to act as cautioner for her husband (ie guarantor for his debts), with the family home being used as a security. The husband reneged on his debts and, unless Mrs Smith could escape the cautionary obligation, the family home would be lost. She proved that her husband had deceived her as to the nature of the cautionary obligation.

The House of Lords held that since the creditor knew of the relationship between the debtor (Mr Smith) and the cautioner (Mrs Smith) they could be taken to be aware of the risk that the one had unduly influenced the other and so the creditor could not enforce the security unless it had taken steps to warn the cautioner of the risks and advised her to take independent legal advice. Mrs Smith was not so warned or advised, therefore the creditor was in bad faith and so unable to enforce the security. Mrs Smith kept her home.

Dudgeon v UK (1981). Northern Irish law prohibited sexual activity between males. Mr Dudgeon, though he had not himself been prosecuted for any offence, had been questioned about his sexual orientation, in an insulting manner, by the police. The European Court held that the criminalisation of all male–male sexual activity was an infringement of Mr Dudgeon's right to private life.

Da Silva Mouta v Portugal (2001). A man sought custody of his daughter against the maternal grandparents but the Portuguese supreme court denied him custody because he was gay. "The child needs a Portuguese, not a gay, upbringing", that court declared. The father took the matter to the European Court of Human Rights and, for the first time, that court held that sexual orientation was an illegitimate ground for discriminating against a person. Though sexual orientation is not mentioned in Article 14, it is nevertheless implicitly included. Subsequent cases have held that the state has the onus of justifying any difference of treatment based on sexual orientation, and that the onus is just as heavy as when a state attempts to justify a difference of treatment based on gender.

Baker v Vermont (1999). The constitution of Vermont has a strong anti-discrimination clause and a number of same-sex couples sought to use that clause to have declared invalid the common law rule that marriage is restricted to relationships between a man and a woman. The onus was on the state to provide rational justification to exclude same-sex couples from the rights and responsibilities of marriage.

The court held that the state had not discharged its onus in providing such a rational justification and that therefore the state was obliged to amend its law to allow a mechanism for same-sex couples to access the rights and responsibilities of marriage. The state of Vermont subsequently did so by introducing by statute civil unions for same-sex couples.

Goodridge v Massachusetts (2003). The constitution of Massachusetts has a strong anti-discrimination clause and a number of same-sex couples sought to use that clause to have declared invalid the common law rule that marriage is restricted to relationships between a man and a woman. The onus was on the state to provide rational justification to exclude same-sex couples from the rights and responsibilities of marriage.

The court held that the state had not discharged its onus in providing such a rational justification and that therefore the state was obliged to amend its law to permit same-sex couples to marry. The state went back to the court and asked "Do you mean we have to let same-sex couples *marry*? Can't we just let them enter into civil unions?". The court answered: "Yes, No" respectively.

7   UNREGISTERED COUPLES

Of course not all couples who live together in a conjugal relationship want to register that relationship with the state. Many couples are technically "unmarried" or are not "civil partners" registered as such, but nevertheless lead their lives in a way that is, to all intents and purposes, indistinguishable from that led by those couples who are registered with the state. Such couples are called "cohabiting couples" and the parties thereto should be referred to as "cohabitants" (and not, as is common, "cohabitees"). Since most of the consequences of marriage and civil partnership discussed above are conferred in recognition of the status conferred by the state, it is right and proper that they are not extended to cohabitants. Many people eschew the very concept of marriage or civil partnership; some prefer to regulate the consequences of their own relationships without the state telling them what consequences there are to be; and a good few people who have been married and did not like the legal consequences thereof (or perhaps did not like the legal and financial consequences of divorce or dissolution) prefer now to enter into domestic relationships over which they have more personal control. In these circumstances it is perfectly justifiable for the law not to provide the full gamut of marital consequences, and this does not amount to discrimination against unregistered couples. For many the choice is theirs and if they want all the legal consequences described in the previous chapter to apply to their relationship then they are free to register it. Of course some couples cannot register, for example because they are not free to marry or enter into a civil partnership, but that too is not discrimination, for that lack of freedom is nearly always justified by good social policy, such as preventing child marriages or bigamous marriages.

There are, however, a number of consequences, mostly of a protective nature, that the law does give to couples who are cohabitants. Before examining these consequences it is important to be aware of what the law understands by cohabitation.

The meaning of "cohabitation " and "cohabitants"

The consequences about to be discussed are virtually all contained within the terms of particular Acts and it follows that the couples covered by the statute will be defined by the statute itself. They all use phrases like "living together as husband and wife" and "living together in a relationship with the characteristics of civil partners" and that is generally as far as the law goes in identifying when a couple will become a cohabitating couple. There are two main elements here. First, the couple must "live together". It is to be noted, in this context, that it is no part of the definition of marriage or civil partnership that the registered partners live together. It is not unknown (and particularly so in the lesbian and gay community) for couples who see themselves as conjugal "couples" to retain separate houses and to live apart. If they do they are not "cohabitants" in the eyes of the law. Second, the relationship must be characterised by the elements that are common for husbands and wives and for civil partners. The unregistered couple must share their lives together in the way that is traditional for registered couples: that is to say must share mutual interests, a social life, be economically interdependent, and be regarded as a member of the other's wider family. As the marital relationship is a relationship based upon sex, so living together as husband and wife requires that the couple's relationship be, or at least have been at an earlier stage, sexually intimate. Many statutes explicitly extend the phrase "living together as husband and wife" to same-sex couples (who, literally, cannot live together as husband and wife because these words refer to a man and a woman); but the House of Lords held in 2004 that even where the statute does not do so the court will read in such an extension if a failure to do so would mean that same-sex couples were treated in a manner unjustifiably discriminatory in relation to opposite-sex couples.

The legal consequences of cohabitation

The legal consequences of a couple whose relationship is unregistered but who are living together as if they were married or in a civil partnership are as follows:

(a) Certain rights to occupy the family home, analogous to those for spouses and civil partners, can be obtained by cohabitants under the Matrimonial Homes (Family Protection) (Scotland) Act 1981 and the Civil Partnership Act 2004. The right of occupancy is not, however, the same and there are three differences from the rights of spouses and civil partners. First, the right of cohabitants is not automatic and must be applied for in court. Second, the right if granted by the court is time limited to 6 months (though it may be extended on an unlimited number of occasions) rather than lasting, as with registered relationships, until the legal end of the relationship. And third, and perhaps most crucially, the right if granted is not good against third parties – in other words, the owner of the property can defeat his or her (ex-)partner's right granted by the court by the simple expedient of selling the property.

(b) Protection from domestic violence: the rules for interdicts and powers of arrest discussed above in relation to married couples and civil partners apply without substantive variation to those in unregistered relationships.

(c) Just as a spouse or civil partner can seek damages on the negligently caused death of their partner under the Damages (Scotland) Act 1976, so too on the same terms and conditions can a cohabitant whose partner is negligently killed.

(d) On the death of a tenant, his or her cohabitant is entitled to succeed to the tenancy, whether it is in the public sector (Housing (Scotland) Act 1988) or the private sector (Housing (Scotland) Act 2001).

(e) Succession rights on death. Since the coming into force of s 29 of the Family Law (Scotland) Act 2006, cohabitants have had limited succession rights in each other's estates. If a cohabitant dies intestate (ie without a valid will) the survivor may ask the court to allocate some or all of the estate to him or her. This is not a claim of right, but a matter for the court's discretion, taking account of all the factors of the case, including other claims on the estate, any benefits (insurance, pensions and the like) that the survivor acquires as a result of his or her partner's death, and the size and nature of the estate. In no circumstances will the survivor be awarded more than he or she would have inherited had he or she been married to or a civil partner of the deceased. And if the deceased was, while cohabiting with the survivor, still in fact married or in a civil partnership with someone else, the surviving spouse or civil partner takes their prior rights and legal rights before the cohabitant's claim is determined.

(f) Financial claims on separation. Also introduced by the Family Law (Scotland) Act 2006 are claims for financial readjustment between the parties when they separate before death (ie they "split up"). These claims are much more limited than those available to spouses or civil partners, described in Chapter 10 below. A "s 28 claim" allows either ex-cohabitant to seek from the other a lump sum or such amount as may be specified, in one of two circumstances. First, a lump sum may be claimed to redress any imbalance in the financial and non-financial contributions of the cohabitants, economic advantages gained from, and economic disadvantages suffered as a result of, the cohabitation. If one cohabitant, in other words, has contributed more, or suffered more, or one has benefited more, than the other (in either financial or other terms) then a lump sum can be claimed to restore the equilibrium between the parties. Second, such amount as may be specified by the court may be awarded in respect of the economic burden of caring, after the end of the cohabitation, for a child under 16 of whom the cohabitants are parents. So the parent with whom the child continues to reside can claim a share of his or her future costs from the other parent who is no longer living with them.

Essential Facts

- A cohabiting couple is a couple who are "living together as husband and wife or as civil partners".
- A cohabitant's claims for occupancy rights differ from those of a spouse or civil partner because they are not automatic, they last only 6 months if granted, and they are not good against third parties.
- The court may make an award of a portion of a deceased's estate to the surviving cohabitant, but the claim is postponed to any claim of a surviving spouse or civil partner.
- The court may make an award of a capital sum from one ex-cohabitant to the other if this is necessary to rebalance any contributions made or disadvantages suffered for the benefit of the relationship, or in order to share the future child-care costs.

Essential Cases

Grant v Edwards (1986). Linda and George lived together for over 20 years, he working, she staying at home, keeping house and bringing up their children. The house was in George's name alone.

The relationship broke down and Linda was unable to seek financial provision on divorce because there could be no divorce since they were never, in fact, married.

The English court held that George held the house on "constructive trust" for the benefit of both himself and Linda. She could therefore claim half its value: an appropriate return for 20 years of washing his socks and dirty underwear, perhaps.

Armour v Anderson (1994). Armour and Anderson lived together but Anderson was violent and Armour fled for her own safety. After some months she sought occupancy rights under the 1981 Act. Anderson's defence was that since Armour had fled she had terminated the cohabitation (which was a matter of fact) and therefore she was no longer a cohabitant and not entitled to seek cohabitants' occupancy rights.

The court rejected this defence and held that the time to determine whether a relationship of cohabitation exists is the time of the event that led to the court action, ie the event that led to Armour fleeing. Any other interpretation would mean that the Act's protective intent could never be given effect to.

Shilliday v Smith (1998). Isobel Shilliday and William Smith commenced living together and became engaged to be married. A house was purchased for them to live in but title was taken in the name of William alone. Nevertheless, Isobel paid for the renovations of the house. The marriage was called off and Isobel claimed back her money on the basis of unjustified enrichment.

The court held that the money should be repaid. The factor that made the enrichment "unjust" was that Isobel had paid the money in the expectation of getting married. When that expectation was frustrated it would be unjust to allow William to keep the benefit of the renovations to his house without cost.

Fitzpatrick v Sterling Housing Association (1999). John Thomson and Martin Fitzpatrick were a gay couple who had lived together for over 20 years in the house rented from a housing association by John. After a long illness John died and Martin sought to succeed to the tenancy. The Rent Act 1977 allowed the survivor of a couple who had "lived together as husband and wife" to succeed, as well as the survivor who was a member of the tenant's family. The landlord denied that John and Martin fulfilled either of these criteria: they could not be a "family" because they were gay.

The House of Lords held that a same-sex couple could not be said to "live together as husband and wife" but that they could be said to be "family". So Martin was able to remain living in his house (and the dam was burst for the full recognition of gay family rights in the UK).

Ghaidan v Mendoza (2004). This case differed from *Fitzpatrick* in that one of the gay couple died after the coming into force of the Human Rights Act 1998.

The House of Lords held that the phrase "living together as husband and wife" had now to be interpreted in a way that was not contrary to Articles 8 and 14 of the European Convention, which prohibited discrimination on the basis of sexual orientation. It was possible to read the phrase to include couples of the same sex who led their lives as married couples and so the survivor was able to succeed to the tenancy not only as a family member but also as a person who lived with the deceased "as husband or wife".

8 DEREGISTERING RELATIONSHIPS BY DIVORCE OR DISSOLUTION

Marriage and civil partnership are matters of legal status while cohabitation is a mere matter of fact: the status is acquired on registration of the relationship. It follows that to escape from the legal consequences of cohabitation one simply needs to change the facts: that is to say, stop cohabiting. But to escape from the legal consequences of marriage or civil partnership one must go through a legal process to remove the legal status, to "deregister", if you like. For marriage the process of deregistration is called divorce and for civil partnership the process is called dissolution. The grounds are substantially, but not exactly, the same.

In modern Scots law there are only two grounds for divorce or dissolution: the obtaining of a gender recognition certificate by one of the partners (ie their having had their sex-change formally recognised), or the irretrievable breakdown of the relationship (Divorce (Scotland) Act 1976, s 1(1); Civil Partnership Act 2004, s 117). The statutes go on to state when, but only when, irretrievable breakdown has occurred and if the facts specified exist then the marriage or civil partnership has broken down in the eyes of the law (irrespective of whether the actual relationship has or not), and if the facts specified do not exist then the marriage or civil partnership has not broken down in the eyes of the law (irrespective of whether the actual relationship survives or not). There are four sets of facts which will deem a marriage to have broken down irretrievably (or to put it more accurately there are four sets of facts which justify a divorce); and there are three sets of facts which will deem a civil partnership to have broken down irretrievably and will justify a dissolution.

Adultery

Adultery is sexual intercourse by a married person with another person not his or her spouse. This is the only ground for divorce that does not also give a ground to dissolve a civil partnership. It is organ-specific and it requires the insertion of a penis into a vagina. Any other sexual act is not adultery and so same-sex sexual activity or any opposite-sex sexual activity other than full penile penetration of the vagina is not in itself absolute proof that the marriage has broken down irretrievably. The adultery must have occurred since the date of the marriage, and one event is sufficient to destroy the marriage. There are a number of defences to an action for divorce based on adultery. First, it is a defence if the pursuer has connived in the act (Divorce (Scotland) Act 1976, s 1(3) which gives statutory effect to the common law defence known as *lenocinium*). This is to prevent parties from seeking an immediate divorce from each other by deciding together that one will provide a ground for the other to use: parties who agree to divorce ought not (in the eyes of the law) to be allowed to do so immediately and they are forced to wait a year – see below). Second, if the pursuer has condoned the act of adultery by the defender then he or she cannot use that act as a ground for divorce. Condonation at common law was forgiveness and though the word "condonation" continues to be used by the statute, actual forgiveness is no longer the issue. Rather, "condonation" is proved by the pursuer cohabiting or continuing to cohabit with the defender three months after cohabiting at any point after discovering the fact of the adultery (Divorce (Scotland) Act 1976, s 2(2) and (4)). Though the wording of the statute is obscure, the rule is not that condonation is created by three months of continuous cohabitation. The length of cohabitation is irrelevant, so long as there is cohabitation at two points in time: one after the discovery of the adultery, and the second at any point after three months after that initial period of cohabitation. Condonation, like *lenocinium*, bars the divorce on this ground.

Unreasonable behaviour

This ground applies to both marriage and civil partnership, though in truth it is not the behaviour that needs to be unreasonable. The actual ground is that the defender has acted in such a way that the pursuer cannot reasonably be expected to continue to cohabit with the defender. So it is the expectation of continued cohabitation rather than the behaviour itself that needs to be shown to be unreasonable. The behaviour that would justify a divorce or dissolution may be something that the defender cannot be blamed for, for example behaviour as a result of a mental illness. And it may be either active or passive, though the difference between passive behaviour and non-behaviour is sometimes not very clear. For example, there would seem to be little doubt that refusing to speak to one's spouse or civil partner would be passive behaviour; but it might be that failing ever to give birthday, anniversary or other special occasion presents is non-behaviour and so not relevant for this ground of divorce or dissolution. Examples of active behaviour would include physical violence towards the other, non-physical behaviour such as verbal abuse, habitual drunkenness even when not resulting in violence, persistent lying, excessive demands for sex, refusal of any sex, knowingly false accusations against the other.

Non-cohabitation with consent

If the defender consents to the divorce or dissolution then the marriage or civil partnership has irretrievably broken down once a year has passed during which the parties did not live together as husband and wife or as civil partners. It frequently happens that within volatile relationships, or after an initial separation, the parties get back together again to see whether they can patch up their differences and recommence their conjugal life together. It would be bad social policy if the law did anything to discourage this, such as by threatening to have the period of a year start running again if the reconciliation attempt fails. So the Divorce (Scotland) Act 1976 and the Civil Partnership Act 2004 allow parties to live together as husband and wife or as civil partners for a period or periods of up to 6 months without interrupting the running of the 1-year period. Of course the time that the couple spend together does not count towards the one year, but it does not stop it and require the whole period to be recommenced. So, for example, if a couple separate on 1 January, attempt reconciliation by moving back together on 1 August, but permanently separate on 1 September, the ground of divorce or dissolution based on 1 year's non-cohabitation with consent to the termination of the relationship is acquired 1 year and 1 month after the initial separation, that is to say in our example 13 months after 1 January.

Non-cohabitation without consent

If the defender refuses to agree to the divorce or dissolution, and no other ground for termination exists, the pursuer must wait until there have been 2 years in which the parties did not live together as husband and wife or as civil partners. As with the 1 year period, the parties are entitled, without losing this ground for divorce or dissolution, to live together for up to 6 months, which period or periods will not count toward the 2 years.

Essential Facts

- Adultery and unreasonable behaviour justify an immediate divorce; the latter also justifies the immediate dissolution of a civil partnership.
- Connivance at, or condonation of, the other's adultery deprives a pursuer of this ground for divorce.
- It is, in reality, not the behaviour that needs to be unreasonable but the continued expectation that the other spouse or civil partner should continue to live with someone who behaves that way.
- Non-cohabitation for 1 year with the consent of the other or non-cohabitation for 2 years without consent are the two no-fault grounds of divorce and dissolution.

Essential Cases

Hunter v Hunter (1900). Mrs Hunter's husband had deserted her and run off to Canada and had not contacted her for a period of time. So she presumed he was dead and contracted a new 'marriage' with her cousin.

When the husband reappeared, he sought a divorce on the basis of her adultery. Mrs Hunter's defence was that she had no *mens rea* for this matrimonial offence since she believed her husband was dead. The court, however, formed the opinion that she had been lax in not obtaining a divorce which she had been legally entitled to as her husband had deserted her. She was therefore held to be guilty of adultery and the divorce was granted.

Hunter v Hunter (1883). Mrs Hunter had been a prostitute before Mr Hunter made a respectable woman of her. During the course of an argument, Mr Hunter shouted at her: "go back to your old ways". She did. She was then sued for divorce on the basis of her adultery and her defence (*lenocinium*) was that Mr Hunter had encouraged her to have sexual relations outwith marriage. The defence failed on the basis that Mr Hunter had spoken *in rixa*, or in anger, and he did not therefore intend to be taken seriously. His words were not a genuine encouragement to commit adultery.

Thomson v Thomson (1908). A wife asked her husband for money to go on an innocent day trip; in fact, she was planning to meet her lover. Her duplicitous husband knew this (though she did not know that he knew) and he gave her the money in the hope that she would meet the lover, commit adultery, and so give him a ground for divorce. The wife took the money, committed adultery, and when her husband sued her for divorce she pleaded *lenocinium*: she claimed that by knowingly giving her the wherewithal to meet the lover Mr Thomson was actively encouraging her to commit adultery.

The court rejected this defence on the basis that the wife did not understand herself to be acting upon the husband's encouragement (ie there was no collusion since the wife was deceived as to the husband's motives).

Gallacher v Gallacher (1928) and Gallacher v Gallacher (1934). A husband wrote to his estranged wife telling her to give him grounds to divorce her. At that time, only desertion (not applicable since the parties were already separated) and adultery were grounds so the letter was really saying "commit adultery". In response, Mrs Gallacher entered into a relationship with another man and when she was sued for divorce she pleaded *lenocinium,* that is to say the encouragement of the letter.

The court (in 1928) held that the letter did indeed amount to encouragement and her adultery was a response to that encouragement and therefore the defence succeeded and the divorce was withheld.

The wife continued to have sex with her new lover and her husband sued her again. And again she pleaded the defence of *lenocinium.*

This time (1934) the defence failed since her sexual actions were no longer a response to the original letter but were a response to her own libidinous desires.

MacLennan v MacLennan (1958). Mrs MacLennan left her husband and went to the USA for some months. When she returned to Scotland she was found to be pregnant and her husband sued her for divorce for adultery. Her defence was that she had become pregnant through artificial insemination and so could not be sued for adultery, which required sexual intercourse.

The court agreed with that defence (though in fact the divorce was granted since she did not prove her story). The case is remembered for Lord Wheatley's description of adultery as being "physical contact with an alien and unlawful sexual organ".

Lennie v Lennie (1950). Mr and Mrs Lennie lived together but Mrs Lennie refused to permit sexual relations. Mr Lennie sued her for divorce on the basis that this amounted to desertion (withdrawal from living together as husband and wife) which until 2006 was another ground of divorce.

The court held that there was more to living together as husband and wife than sexual relations and that the termination (even by one party against the wishes of the other) of sexual relations was not in itself sufficient to amount to desertion.

White v White (1966). Mr White was caught by police, having sex with another man in a public toilet. His wife sued him for divorce on the basis of cruelty (since gay sex does not amount to adultery). His defence was that since the action was not directed to his wife it could not be said to amount to cruelty.

The court rejected this defence and held that the behaviour was cruel because it had effects on the wife, even when not directed to her. (Cruelty is no longer a ground for divorce, having been replaced in 1976 by the wider concept of unreasonable behaviour.)

Hastie v Hastie (1985). Mr and Mrs Hastie separated and were involved in a bitter custody dispute over who would get their daughter. In the course of that dispute Mrs Hastie made an allegation that her husband had committed incest with their daughter. She later admitted that she had invented this, in order to ruin her opponent's chances in the custody dispute.

The court held that though a single event, this deliberately false allegation was so destructive of the marital relationship that it amounted to behaviour such that it was unreasonable to expect the pursuer to continue living with the defender. Mr Hastie was granted a divorce on that basis.

Findlay v Findlay (1991). Mr Findlay kept late hours and Mrs Findlay did not like it. This was not, however, sufficient to amount to behaviour such that it was unreasonable to expect her to continue living with her husband and so she did not have any ground to divorce him. But she left him, nevertheless. She subsequently formed an association with another man and at this stage sued her husband for unreasonable behaviour.

The court held that it was unreasonable to expect Mrs Findlay, happy with her new man, to return to Mr Findlay with whom she was unhappy and therefore the ground of divorce was now made out.

9 DEREGISTERING RELATIONSHIPS BY ANNULMENT

If a party to a marriage or civil partnership wishes to escape from their legal relationship but does not for some reason wish to seek a divorce or dissolution, an alternative is to seek to have the marriage or civil partnership annulled instead. In other words, the party may attempt to persuade the court that the marriage or civil partnership never was valid in the first place. It is not possible to found upon minor irregularities in the process of entering into the marriage or civil partnership, such as that the celebrant was not properly authorised, or the place of marriage or civil partnership was not as stated in the marriage notice and marriage schedule. Section 23A of the Marriage (Scotland) Act 1977 provides that irregularities of this nature will be ignored. This is because a marriage or civil partnership is not a contract but is a status and there are strong public policy reasons to uphold marriage and civil partnership from challenges on matters of little social import. However, a marriage or civil partnership can be annulled, that is to say declared never to have been valid, if the irregularity affects an issue that goes to the essence of the status of marriage or civil partnership, such as for example the capacity of the party to enter into it. There are numerous grounds available to a party who wishes to challenge the validity of a marriage or civil partnership.

Age

If the parties are not old enough to marry or register a civil partnership, any purported marriage or civil partnership is null and void. A marriage or civil partnership which takes place in Scotland is valid only if both parties are over the age of 16 (Marriage (Scotland) Act 1977, s 1(2); Civil Partnership Act 2004, s 86(1)(c)), and it does not matter for the application of this rule that one of the parties comes from a country where the age of marriage or civil partnership is lower. And the age of 16 is the age of marriage and civil partnership for all persons domiciled in Scotland no matter where in the world the marriage or civil partnership takes place (Marriage (Scotland) Act 1977, s 1(1); Civil Partnership Act 2004, s 217(4)). It follows that if the marriage took place or the civil partnership was registered in Scotland at any time before either party's 16th birthday, or it took place abroad before the Scottish party's 16th birthday, the marriage or civil partnership is fatally flawed and has no legal effect. A civil partnership involving a Scottish person over the age of 16 cannot take place if the other party is under 16, even in a country with a lower age limit than Scotland. The rule is different with marriage and a 16 year old may marry abroad a 15 year old if the 15 year old's legal system allows this.

Sometimes the age of marriage is 21 in Scotland. A person who wishes to marry or enter a civil partnership with an affinitive relation (defined below) in circumstances in which the law allows this may do so only after they are both 21 years of age or older (Marriage (Scotland) Act 1977, s 2; Civil Partnership Act 2004, s 86(3).)

Forbidden degrees

If the parties to the marriage or civil partnership are within the forbidden degrees of relationship they are incapable of marrying each other or registering a civil partnership with each other (Marriage (Scotland) Act 1977, s 2; Civil Partnership Act 2004, Sch 10), and any purported marriage or civil partnership between parties within these relationships is null and void. There are three categories of forbidden degree: consanguine, adoptive and affinitive.

Consanguine relationships are relationships of blood. A person may not marry or enter into a civil partnership with his or her parent, grandparent, great-grandparent, child, grandchild, great grandchild, sibling, aunt, uncle, niece or nephew. Adoptive relationships are created through an adoption order made by a court of competent jurisdiction. A person may not marry or enter into a civil partnership with his or her adoptive parent or adoptive child (though he or she may do so with any other relative traced through the adoptive parent or child). Affinitive relationships are created through marriage or civil partnership and, unless the exception applies, a person may not marry or enter into a civil partnership with the ex-spouse or civil partner of his or her parent. The exception, permitting marriage or civil partnership within step-relationships, is if the parties never lived in family with each other before the younger reached the age of 18, the older never treated the younger as a child of the family, and they are both now over the age of 21.

Same sex or opposite sex

The law of Scotland treats marriage and civil partnership as fundamentally different institutions, notwithstanding the fact that the legal consequences of each, capacities to enter and rules for exit, are substantially the same. But marriage is limited in its availability to opposite-sex couples while civil partnership is limited in its availability to same-sex couples. It follows from this that a marriage is void if entered into by a same-sex couple (Marriage (Scotland) Act 1977, s 5(4)(e)) and a civil partnership is void if entered into by an opposite-sex couple (Civil Partnership Act 2004, s 86(1)(a)). People who have undergone gender realignment surgery and who live their lives in the opposite gender to that which appears on their birth certificates remain in law the original gender for these purposes until they acquire a gender recognition certificate granted under the terms of the Gender Recognition Act 2004, but once that certificate has been obtained they can marry or enter a civil partnership in their acquired gender.

Existing marriage or civil partnership

Marriage has always been in Scotland, and civil partnership is statutorily, a monogamous relationship and it follows that a party who is already a party to one or other of these institutions may not enter into another one without the first ending (either through death of the partner, or divorce, dissolution or annulment). If they purport to do so, the subsequent marriage or civil partnership is null and void. This is not to say that polygamous marriages validly entered into in another legal system which allows this will not be recognised here as a marriage. Rather, so long as the parties had capacity to enter into a multiple-person relationship and they did so in a country that treats multiple-person relationships as marriage, the parties thereto will be regarded as married in this country for most purposes (Domicile and Matrimonial Proceedings Act 1973, as amended by the Private International Law (Miscellaneous Provisions) Act 1995). No jurisdiction which permits civil partnership has allowed it to be entered into polygynously and so the issue would not arise with civil partners.

Incapacity to understand

The above grounds upon which a marriage or civil partnership can be annulled are relatively straightforward to deal with since the facts at issue are usually very easy to establish. Proof of age or gender or existing relationship is seldom susceptible to doubt or uncertainty. Incapacity to understand, however, is very different for there is much room for uncertainty and different interpretation of the facts that can be proved.

The basic rule is that a person who was at the time of the marriage ceremony or civil partnership registration incapable of understanding the nature of marriage or civil partnership and of consenting thereto is not able for that reason to enter a marriage or civil partnership. Any purported consent is of no effect and the marriage or civil partnership based on such purported consent is null and void. However, it has always been the view of the law that marriage (and the same, presumably, can be said of civil partnership) is a simple concept, easy to understand, and understood by most people even if of very low intelligence. It follows that to escape a marriage or civil partnership on an assertion that one of the parties did not understand its nature, the claimant must show that the party's ability to understand anything is very severely compromised. A person who does not have the intellectual capacity to make a will or enter into a contract may well be able to understand the simple institution of marriage. There is no room for the argument that a person's consent to marriage or civil partnership is void as having been obtained through facility and circumvention (ie simple-mindedness and undue pressure). The onus on the person seeking to have the marriage or civil partnership annulled on this ground is heavy.

It is sometimes argued that a person's consent to marriage or civil partnership has been obtained by fraud, or that the person whose consent is at issue is under a vitiating error of understanding: in these circumstances the court may annul the marriage or civil partnership. But it will be slow to do so and there is no possibility of a marriage or civil partnership being annulled on the basis of error as to the quality of the partner one is acquiring. A woman who marries a man believing him to be rich, and good, does not have an invalid marriage just because she discovers that he has been lying to her and he is destitute, and cruel. A man who marries a woman because he believes that the child she is carrying is his cannot have that marriage annulled on the basis of mistake if he were to discover that the child was in fact fathered by another man. Error is relevant only when it goes to the very identity of the other party or of the nature of the ceremony (Marriage (Scotland) Act 1977, s 20A(5); Civil Partnership Act 2004, s 123(2); both as amended by the Family Law (Scotland) Act 2006). Given that the presence of both at the ceremony of marriage or civil partnership registration is required, error as to identity, while conceivable, is highly unlikely ever to occur in Scotland.

Consent, to be valid, is consent to be married or consent to have a civil partnership registered. Consent to anything else does not make marriage or civil partnership. Occasionally the Scottish court held that if one of the parties, while appearing to consent to marriage, is not in fact agreeing to enter into the lawful status of marriage with the other person but is consenting only to the obtaining of some extraneous benefit (for example immigration) then the marriage can be declared null for lack of consent. This was a dangerous doctrine but "tacitly withholding consent" was abolished as a ground upon which a marriage or civil partnership could be annulled by the Family Law (Scotland) Act 2006, s 2 and Sch 1).

However, if a person is forced into marriage against his or her will, and has given consent only through fear of bodily or mental injury, then their consent is not genuine and the marriage or civil partnership may be annulled for lack of consent. There is here an important (though sometimes subtle) difference between an arranged marriage (which is legitimate) and a forced marriage (which is not). The issue is unlikely to arise in the context of civil partnership.

Impotency

There is one ground for having a marriage annulled that does not apply to civil partnership. And this ground is unique even within marriage in that it presupposes a valid marriage at the time it was entered into, but which can be retrospectively annulled if one or other of the parties seeks to have it annulled: unless and until this happens, the marriage is valid (unlike any of the other grounds whereby the marriage or civil partnership is held to be void from the beginning, or void *ab initio*). The marriage is therefore not void but merely voidable. In reality this is divorce by pretending the marriage never was, and is important for those who do not believe in, but want to benefit from, divorce. The ground is the incurable impotency of one or other of the parties at the time of the marriage. Impotency, like adultery, is organ-specific and is the inability (whether caused by mental inhibition or physical incapacity) to achieve full penile penetration of the vagina. Ability or inability to indulge in any other sort of sexual activity is not relevant. Ability or inability to achieve full sexual intercourse with another person is not relevant. Ability or inability to have children is not relevant. Impotency is no more nor any less than the inability to achieve full penile penetration of the vagina with one's marriage partner. Impotency, to be relevant, must exist at the date of the marriage, and it must be at that point in time incurable (though scientific developments providing a cure subsequently is also irrelevant).

Civil partnership does not require the ability of one partner to penetrate in a sexual manner any part of the other's body before the relationship is complete and unchallengeable.

Essential Facts

- Marriage and civil partnership can only be entered into in Scotland if both parties are over the age of 16 years; Scottish domiciliaries may not marry nor enter into a marriage or civil partnership anywhere in the world before their 16th birthday.
- The forbidden degrees of marriage and civil partnership are: (a) parent, child, grandparent, grandchild, great-grandparent, great-grandchild, brother, sister, uncle, aunt, nephew and niece; (b) adoptive or former adoptive parent, adoptive or former adoptive child; (c) step-parent, stepchild. There are some exceptions to (c) but none to (a) or (b).
- Marriage and civil partnership may only be entered into in the UK monogamously; UK law might, however, recognise foreign polygamous marriages.
- You take your partner for better or for worse, so your consent is not vitiated by any error you make about the quality of your partner, except his or her identity.
- Consent to marriage or civil partnership may be vitiated if it has been obtained by duress, with threats to physical or mental wellbeing.
- A marriage (but not a civil partnership) is voidable (ie valid until challenged) if one of the parties was incurably impotent at the time of the marriage.

Essential Cases

F v F (1945). Mr F raised an action against his wife, seeking to have their marriage declared a nullity on the ground of his own incurable impotency at the date of the wedding. In the past actions had only been raised by the potent partner against the impotent partner. But the court held that it was only third parties who were excluded from raising actions based on impotency and so there was nothing to prevent Mr F seeking nullity of marriage on the basis of his own impotency.

Hastings v Hastings (1941). Alice Hastings had induced her husband to marry her on the false pretext that she was carrying his child. Mr Hastings, on discovering he had been trapped into the marriage, refused to cohabit with her and raised an action of declarator and the child was declared illegitimate. Mrs Hastings then raised an action for divorce for his apparent desertion, hoping that she, as any wife who has divorced her husband for desertion, could claim a share of his estate. The divorce was refused as her husband's desertion was not "without reasonable cause".

Lang v Lang (1921). Walter Lang, seaman from Leith, was invited by Violette Pieroni, spinster of that parish, to spend the night with her. He did so, and repeated the experience on numerous occasions, and when informed by Violette that she was pregnant, he married her. In fact, Violette had been having sex with someone else before Seaman Lang came along and the child was not her husband's. He sought a declarator of invalidity of marriage on the basis that his consent was based on a false premise, that the child was his.

The court held that consent given in error as to the quality of the other party is irrelevant, but error as to the identity of the other will render the consent invalid. Declarator of invalidity was refused.

Corbett v Corbett (1971). George Jamieson became April Ashley and married Arthur Corbett. When that relationship collapsed, April sued for divorce and Arthur pleaded the marriage was null and void as having been between two men.

The court held that April was not "female" for the purposes of marriage since she could not perform "the essential role of a woman" in marriage, which was to provide a natural and not artificial vagina for the satisfaction of her husband.

Bellinger v Bellinger (2003). Mr and Mrs Bellinger had been married for 20 years, Mr Bellinger having entered into the marriage fully aware that Mrs Bellinger had been born male and had undergone gender reassignment surgery. They sought a declaration that their marriage was valid.

The House of Lords accepted that *Corbett* continued to represent English law and that biological factors determined gender for the purposes of marriage. It followed that Mr and Mrs Bellinger were both men and the marriage was void. They issued, however, a declaration of incompatibility with the ECHR since the European Court had earlier held the *Corbett* rule to be contrary to both Articles

8 and 12 (*Goodwin* v *United Kingdom* (2002) 35 EHRR18). The Gender Recognition Act 2004 reversed the result of this case (and, of course, of *Corbett*).

McLeod v Adams (1920). Mrs Christina McLeod was a war widow with five young children. She was seduced by Robert Adams who claimed to be a soldier with a regular salary. Unfortunately he was a rogue. He persuaded her to marry him and then made off with her life savings. She was left in penury, her war widow's pension having been withdrawn on her remarriage. She now sought a declarator of invalidity of marriage on the basis that he had not really consented to "marry" her but had consented merely to a form of union that would entitle him to access her money: he had, in other words, an unexpressed "mental reservation" to the marriage which took away the validity of his consent.

The court, sympathetic to Christina, granted the declarator of invalidity of marriage and restored her status as a widow rather than a deserted wife. The effect of this decision was reversed by the Family Law (Scotland) Act 2006, s 2(4).

Mahmud v Mahmud (1994). Shahid Mahmud lived with his girlfriend Lesley Scott and their child. His parents arranged for him to marry his cousin, whom they imported from Pakistan for the purpose. Though initially he refused, he eventually gave in to the family pressure put upon him (he was threatened that shame and degradation would be visited upon the whole family unless he submitted to the marriage arranged by his parents). Immediately after the marriage ceremony, he returned home to Lesley and their child. The wife was soon thereafter deported back from whence she came (where she led a humiliated life, unmarriable but without a husband). Shahid now sought a declarator of nullity on the basis that his consent had been forced from him through the duress of his family.

Lord Prosser held that his will had been overborne and his consent was vitiated, with the result that the marriage was null and void.

Singh v Singh (2005). June Kaur was 18 years old, with a boyfriend called Keith Singh, when her mother took her to India and married her off, against her will, to a man she did not know, called Bikramjit

Singh. June was taken to her new husband's house but she refused to have sex with him and a week later she returned home to Scotland. She moved out of her parents' house and went to live with Keith. She now sought a declarator that she had not given valid consent to her marriage which was, therefore, void.

The court found that June's mother had threatened to destroy her passport, leaving her stranded in India, if she did not submit. It held that this threat of immediate danger to June's liberty, causing her will to be overborne, vitiated her consent. But the judge also sounded a cautionary note. The threats had to be of immediate danger to life, limb or liberty. He doubted whether the threats in the earlier case of *Mahmud* v *Mahmud* (above) satisfied this test.

10 FINANCIAL PROVISION ON DIVORCE, DISSOLUTION AND ANNULMENT

Whenever a court brings a marriage or civil partnership to an end, whether by divorce, dissolution or annulment, it is empowered to make orders for financial readjustment between the parties. In other words, the court is entitled to order one ex-partner to transfer some of their property or make a cash payment to the other ex-partner, and even to make a periodical payment thereto. Prior to the Family Law (Scotland) Act 1985 the court's power to do so at the end of a marriage was virtually unlimited and exercised extremely narrowly: the spousal obligation of aliment was continued on divorce by requiring the wealthier ex-spouse (nearly always the ex-husband) to make a periodical allowance to the other, which was to last for the rest of the life of the other (or until her remarriage and acquisition thereby of another source of support). There were a number of unfortunate consequences to this. First, it maintained a relationship between the parties after the end of their marriage though that relationship was reduced to one of pure financial giving and taking. Second, it encouraged the receiver to expect to continue to receive and did nothing to encourage her (and it usually was a woman) to attempt to regain a position of independence. The 1985 Act attempted to change all that by introducing into the law the philosophy of the "clean break". Now, on divorce, dissolution or annulment, the court is encouraged to deal with the parties' joint finances in a "once and for all" manner, in order to even out the financial inequities that are inevitable in many relationships and to put both parties on the road to financial independence, rather than to ensure that one continues to be able to rely on the other for life. A periodical allowance may still be made, but only when it is proved that a "once and for all" settlement is inappropriate in the special circumstances of the case or is inadequate.

The court has the power to make a range of orders, including an order requiring a property owner to transfer items of property to his or her ex-partner, requiring one party to make a financial payment to the other, an order splitting the pension fund of one so that the other has a pension too, requiring the payment on a regular basis of a periodical allowance to the other, and various incidental orders such as valuation and sale of property (Family Law (Scotland) Act 1985, s 8(1)). Before any order can be made by the court two separate tests must be satisfied. First, the order must be reasonable having regard to the resources of the parties. So it will seldom be appropriate to order one ex-partner to pay over all they have to the other, or to require them to make a periodical allowance greater than their own income. Second, and far more problematic, the order must be justified by one of the principles laid down in s 9(1) of the 1985 Act (the "s 9 Principles"). In other words, in order to make a claim for financial provision on divorce, dissolution or annulment, the claimant must justify that claim by reference to one or more of the s 9 Principles. A claim will not be relevant if justified on any other basis. But even where a claim can be justified by one or more of the s 9 Principles, the court retains the final discretion and may not, in the circumstances of the case, make any order at all.

However, notwithstanding its discretion, 20 years of application of the Act has shown that the Scottish courts will treat the application of the first principle (fair sharing of matrimonial property) as virtually a claim of right which every divorcing or dissolving couple should expect to receive or to pay; the other principles may be applied in the particular circumstances of the case, or it may be regarded that the payment made under the first principle also satisfies any claim that can be justified by any of the other principles.

Fair sharing of matrimonial property

The first of the s 9 Principles is contained in s 9(1)(a) of the 1985 Act and it is that "the net value of the matrimonial property should be shared fairly between the parties to the marriage". This apparently simple statement is full of legal complication, which students must grasp since this Principle is far and away the most important of them all. There are four concepts contained within the Principle that need discussing.

Net value
Net value is the value of the property subject to deduction of debts due upon the property. The easiest case is that of the family home that is subject to a mortgage. If, for example, the parties live in a house valued at £150,000 but there is a mortgage of £100,000 on the property then the net value, available for sharing, is £50,000. While that is straightforward, what has proved difficult for the court is the process of valuation. There is often a difference between the price one party's valuers put on an item of property and the price the other party's valuers put on it, for valuation is seldom an exact and predictable science. As a general rule it is for the claimant to establish to the court the accuracy of the valuation he or she

claims a share of. Value is sometimes affected by whose eyes it is seen from. The market value of a house or a business may not be the "value" that a seller receives for it, if, for example, there is a charge to capital gains tax when it is sold, or some other penalty is accrued on its sale (such as, for example, repaying the discount received when an ex-council house tenant has bought their home and subsequently sells it). The Court of Session resolved many years of doubt in 2003 by holding that "value" for the purpose of the 1985 Act is market value and not the net profit gained by the person who disposes of the property.

The relevant date

Another difficulty with "net value" is the date upon which it is valued. The statute makes plain that the property that is to be shared fairly under this principle is the net value at "the relevant date" which is, basically, the date the parties finally separated (though the precise date can sometimes be disputed if parties gradually drift apart). And since the relevant date can often be some years prior to the actual action for divorce it may be that the property substantially increases or decreases in value. In that situation it is still the value at the date of separation that is to be shared, for that is all that is justified by s 9(1)(a). So if partners separate in 2006 and there is a house with a net worth of £110,000 at that time, but when they seek dissolution of their civil partnership in 2009 the house has a net worth of £160,000, s 9(1)(a) justifies only the fair sharing of £110,000. If the financial provision that the court decides to make is to order a transfer of property that has increased in its value, then sometimes the value at the date of transfer rather than the relevant date will be used for that purpose (Family Law (Scotland) Act 2006, s 16, amending the 1985 Act). But the "relevant date" rule can work both ways. If a husband owns shares worth £50,000 at the relevant date but on the date of divorce they are now worth £25,000, his ex-wife would in principle be entitled under s 9(1)(a) to receive shares worth half of £50,000, even although that is no longer half of what the ex-husband now owns. The potential unfairness of that is ameliorated by the power of the court to take account of available resources.

Matrimonial property

The most difficult part of this principle is the concept of matrimonial property itself (called "partnership property" for the purposes of civil partnership). The key to understanding s 9(1)(a) is to recognise that the principle contained therein justifies a fair sharing of only that property that comes within the highly technical definition of "matrimonial property": this is *not* all the property the parties own, either jointly or singly, but only that property coming within the definition contained in s 10(4) of the 1985 Act. The parties are very likely to own other property than "matrimonial property" but if an ex-partner wants a share of that other property on divorce, dissolution or annulment, he or she must justify that claim by a Principle other than that contained in s 9(1)(a).

Section 10(4) defines "matrimonial property" as all the property belonging to the parties or either of them at the relevant date which was acquired by them or him or her (otherwise than by way of gift or succession from a third party) during the marriage or civil partnership but before the relevant date. The moment of acquisition is crucial here. Property becomes "matrimonial property" (and therefore available for fair sharing under s 9(1)(a)) if it was acquired by either party at some point in time between the moment the legal relationship is established (the date of the marriage or of the registration of the civil partnership) and the relevant date. So, property owned by the parties before the marriage or civil partnership is not (subject to an exception mentioned immediately below) "matrimonial property"; property acquired after the relevant date is not "matrimonial property"; property acquired by way of gift or succession from a third party is not "matrimonial property". The exception to the date of acquisition is that property may be "matrimonial property" for this purpose if it was acquired before the marriage or civil partnership, but it was acquired for use by the parties as a family home or as furniture or plenishings for such a home.

The definition is to be applied quite literally, with the result that property that is not originally matrimonial property can become matrimonial property if it has changed its nature in some way. For example, a partner to a marriage or civil partnership may inherit some money during the marriage or civil partnership. That money, as inherited property, cannot be matrimonial property notwithstanding that it was acquired during the marriage or civil partnership (since inherited property is excluded from the definition in s 10(4)). But if the partner uses that money to buy something, such as a house or a car, then the house or car has been acquired during the marriage or civil partnership, it has not been (itself) inherited, and therefore it is "matrimonial property" and available for distribution under the Principle in s 9(1)(a).

Fair sharing

The s 9(1)(a) Principle requires that the net value of the matrimonial property be shared "fairly" between the parties. There is a presumption that fair sharing means equal sharing, with the result that the parties can expect to take away from the marriage or civil partnership 50% of the matrimonial property, irrespective of who, before the divorce, dissolution or annulment, actually owned the property. This equal split of the matrimonial property does not require the court to award half of every item to each party. Rather, the court is seeking a universal figure of the matrimonial property, which is then notionally divided by two to give the figure that each can expect to take. If their ownership of matrimonial property is 50–50 in any case then s 9(1)(a) does not justify any award of financial provision (unless s 10(6), discussed below, applies). If, as will be the usual case, there is a disparity in the shares each own of the matrimonial property, then the Principle justifies the court making an order to transfer half the difference, either in cash or in property. For example, imagine a couple jointly own the family home worth £100,000, each has a car (A owns a car worth £5,000 and B owns a car worth £2,000), and A has shares worth £15,000 (their other property not coming within the definition of matrimonial property). Here, the total matrimonial property is £122,000 and so each can expect to take £61,000 away. Since A already owns £70,000 (half the house, her car and the shares) and B already owns £52,000 (half the house and the other car), a transfer from A to B of £9,000 is required to ensure that each leaves the marriage with the correct amount of £61,000. How A pays this is a matter for negotiation but if the parties cannot agree the court will decide and can require A either to make a cash settlement or to transfer an item of property worth £9,000.

One final point to note in relation to the Principle in s 9(1)(a) is that the statute seeks to achieve a "fair" share rather than an "equal" share. It follows that while equality is presumed to be fair, this presumption can be overturned. So a party can argue that they should receive more than a half or that the other should receive less than a half, on the basis that there are special circumstances justifying this departure from equal sharing. Section 10(6) lists examples of what amounts to special circumstances and includes things like any agreement between the parties as to the division of the matrimonial property, the sources of the funds used to acquire the matrimonial property, any dissipation by one party of matrimonial funds, and the nature of the property, including whether it is used for the business purposes of one of the parties.

The other s 9 Principles

There are four other Principles in s 9(1) of the Family Law (Scotland) Act 1985, each of which may be used to justify a claim for financial provision on divorce, dissolution or annulment of a marriage or civil partnership.

First, fair account should be taken of any economic advantage derived by either party from contributions, whether financial or otherwise, of the other; and of any economic disadvantages suffered by either party in the interests of the other party or of the family (1985 Act, s 9(1)(b)). A partner who gives up a job for the sake of the family (typically, when a woman gives birth and takes time out of her career) suffers an economic disadvantage vis-à-vis her partner who is able to continue working and improving his or her career and this principle is designed to recognise this and allow the court to make such financial provision as will equalise the partners. As with fair sharing of matrimonial property, this principle only justifies a one-off payment of either cash or property, and in determining the appropriate amount the court is able to take account of the extent to which the economic advantages and disadvantages have been evened out by an award justified by the fair sharing of matrimonial property.

Second, any economic burden of caring for a child of the family under the age of 16 years should be shared fairly between the parties (1985 Act, s 9(1)(c)). This refers to the actual costs of bringing up a child and not the minimal obligation of reasonable aliment that an absent parent owes to the child in any case. The residence parent invariably spends substantially more than is absolutely necessary to provide the child with food, shelter and clothing, and this principle justifies the court making an award to the residence parent to ensure that this actual expenditure is shared fairly between the two. Frequently it is satisfied by the court transferring the half share of the family home that belonged, before divorce or dissolution or annulment, to the non-resident parent: this has the added attraction of ensuring that the children are able to continue residing in the home that they are used to. This Principle can justify the court making a periodical allowance as well as a transfer of property, which is sometimes appropriate since child-rearing expenses are ongoing and often unpredictable. However, if a periodical allowance is made, it comes to an end on the child's 16th birthday and so it is not indefinite.

Third, a party who has been dependent to a substantial degree on the financial support of the other party should be awarded such financial provision as is reasonable to enable him or her to adjust, over a period of not more than three years, from the date of the decree, to the loss of that support by the divorce, dissolution or annulment (1985 Act, s 9(1)(d)). This is designed to provide a 3-year cushion to persons who have been long out of the job market and would, therefore, require some retraining before being able to become fully independent. The court will have regard to such matters as the age, health and earning capacity of the party claiming financial provision justified by this Principle, the duration and extent of the claimant's financial dependency, and any intention of the claimant to undergo training. Another matter which the court is able to take into account is the conduct of either party, but only if it would be inequitable to leave it out of account. Generally conduct is irrelevant and the court will not take it into account in determining any of the preceding Principles. Either a one-off payment or a periodical allowance may be made here, but if the latter only for 3 years.

Finally, a party who at the time of the divorce, dissolution or annulment seems likely to suffer serious financial hardship as a result of the divorce should be awarded such financial provision as is reasonable to relieve him or her of hardship over a reasonable period of time (1985 Act, s 9(1)(e)). This is a "safety net" provision designed to ensure that a party on divorce or dissolution does not suffer serious financial hardship which cannot be resolved by any of the other Principles. There may, for example, be very little in the way of matrimonial property and in that situation if one partner is a high earner and the other not, the other may claim that he or she would suffer serious financial hardship by losing the right to claim aliment, or a share of the other's pension, or later succession rights. Though a one-off payment may be made, it is more common for a periodical allowance to be awarded under this Principle and, if so, this is the only Principle that justifies an indefinite periodical allowance. Courts should be aware, however, that whenever they make an indefinite periodical allowance they are going against the main thrust of the 1985 Act, which is to encourage a "clean break"" between the parties. In determining what award to make under this principle, the court may have regard to the age, health and earning capacity of the party claiming financial provision, the standard of living of the parties during the marriage or civil partnership, the needs and resources of the parties and also (as with the Principle discussed immediately above but none of the others) the conduct of the parties if it would be manifestly inequitable to leave that conduct out of account.

Essential Facts

- Financial provision on divorce, dissolution or annulment aims to achieve a "clean break" by preferring a one-off payment from one to the other: this way independence is encouraged.

- On divorce, dissolution or annulment, a claim to 50% of the property acquired during the marriage or civil partnership (called the "matrimonial property" or "partnership property") is virtually a claim of right.
- The matrimonial property is valued at the "relevant date" which is (basically) the date of final separation.
- The 50–50 split of matrimonial property is merely presumed to be fair and either party has the opportunity to justify a different division by proving the existence of special circumstances.
- A claim for financial provision under s 9(1)(b) requires there to have been an imbalance in the contributions made or disadvantages suffered for the good of the relationship.
- A claim for financial provision under s 9(1)(c) may allow actual child-care costs to be shared by way of periodical allowance until the child is 16.

Essential Cases

Skarpass v Skarpass (1991). A s 9(1)(a) claim. Dorothy Skarpass sued her husband, Torsteinn Skarpass, for divorce and she sought financial provision from him. His only asset was an amount of money he had obtained as damages for an accident at work. The damages had been paid after the relevant date, but the accident was suffered before the relevant date. Mr Skarpass claimed that the money, having been obtained after the relevant date, was not matrimonial property; and that in any case since it was damages for a personal injury suffered by him the sharing should not be 50–50 but 100% to him.

The court held that the damages were "matrimonial property" because the right to obtain damages had arisen before the relevant date; that while some departure from a 50–50 split was justified in relation to the portion of the damages referable to solatium, the major portion was for loss of earnings which should be shared 50–50. So Mrs Skarpass was entitled to a share in the damages, though not as much as 50%. However, Mr Skarpass had taken to drink after the accident, reducing the assets available for distribution, and so the sheriff held that, taking this into account, Mrs Skarpass's claim should be brought back up to 50% of the total matrimonial property.

Davidson v Davidson (1994). A s 9(1)(a) claim. Anna Davidson sued her husband, James Davidson, for divorce. At the relevant date, Mrs Davidson owned investments of almost half a million pounds, but this was not matrimonial property. During the marriage Mr and Mrs Davidson purchased a farm, which Mrs Davidson worked. This was the sole item of matrimonial property. Mrs Davidson continued to look after the children and work the farm; Mr Davidson's timber business had failed and he had fallen into ill-health which meant he could no longer work. He sought financial provision: a half share of the farm.

The court held that since the farm had been purchased with money inherited by Mrs Davidson it would be wrong to give Mr Davidson his full claim of one half. But given his impoverished state in comparison to his ex-wife, he ought to receive part of the matrimonial property and an order was made for Mrs Davidson to pay over to her ex-husband an amount representing around one third of the value of the farm.

Whittome v Whittome (No 1) (1994). A s 9(1)(a) claim. Timothy Whittome sued his wife, Beverly Whittome, for divorce and Beverly claimed a half share of the matrimonial property. The issue was whether a shareholding belonging to Timothy was matrimonial property and required to be part of the calculation. The shares were in a private family company (Christian Salvesen) and Timothy had acquired them over the years partly as a gift from his uncle (Mr Norman Salvesen) and partly as payments from various trust funds set up by the Salvesen family. Beverly argued that the company had undergone various reconstitutions and so the original shares that Timothy had acquired by gift and succession were not the shares he now held: rather, he had acquired the current shares directly from the company.

The court held that the shares held by Timothy, issued by the company, were the shares he originally acquired by gift or succession; that the company reconstitutions did not affect this conclusion; and that therefore the shares were not "matrimonial property" to which Beverly had a claim. (It was also held that an increase in the value of non-matrimonial property during the marriage is not in itself matrimonial property.)

Cunniff v Cunniff (1999). A s 9(1)(a) claim. Dorothy Cunniff sued her husband, Kevin Cunniff, for divorce and sought financial provision. Kevin's financial affairs were complex but he was a high earner and was adept at avoiding his liabilities (such as a tax liability to the Irish government). Between the date of separation (the relevant date) and the date of the court action for divorce, Kevin had transferred most of his realisable assets into his pension fund, and at the date of proof the only substantial piece of matrimonial property left was the matrimonial home in which Mrs Cunniff and the youngest child of the marriage continued to live. The house was owned jointly and the financial provision ordered by the Lord Ordinary was to require Mr Cunniff to transfer his half share in the house to his ex-wife. He appealed on the ground that this amounted to Mrs Cunniff receiving virtually 100% of the matrimonial property and to a requirement that he transfer all his realisable property to her.

The Inner House held that the decision of the Lord Ordinary was justified. Mr Cunniff had a valuable pension which was part of the "resources" that the court could take into account in determining whether the outcome was reasonable or not. Transferring all the matrimonial assets from one to the other was also reasonable because Mr Cunniff remained in a high earning position and could easily look after himself even if he ended the marriage with no assets; Mrs Cunniff on the other hand (having been out of the job market for many years) could not so readily earn an income and she had continuing obligations to look after the child.

Sweeney v Sweeney (2004). A s 9(1)(a) claim. Susan Sweeney sued Patrick Sweeney for divorce and sought a share in the extensive matrimonial property owned by her husband. The Lord Ordinary valued the property under deduction of capital gains tax, since Mr Sweeney would have to sell the property to meet Mrs Sweeney's claims and he would be liable to that tax charge. On appeal the Inner House held that the value of the matrimonial property was the value that a purchaser would pay, not the value that a seller would receive, and so the Lord Ordinary had erred in deducting capital gains tax before sharing the remainder between the parties.

Mr Sweeney then cross appealed on the ground that there were special circumstances justifying him in paying to his ex-wife less than 50%. In particular he argued that his remaining assets were business assets and not easily realised. Mrs Sweeney pointed out that since the original decree Mr Sweeney had been busy transferring assets from a realisable nature to a non-realisable nature (ie putting his free funds into his business).

The Inner House held that Mr Sweeney had not acted unreasonably and that the difficulty in realising his assets was indeed a special circumstance justifying a departure from equal sharing. So Mr Sweeney was ordered to pay rather less than half the value of the matrimonial property.

Cahill v Cahill (1998). A s 9(1)(b) claim. Mr Cahill sued Mrs Cahill for divorce and he sought a capital sum under s 9(1)(b) on the basis of contributions he had made. Mrs Cahill owned a cottage which she let out and she did not share the rent with her husband. But Mr Cahill had worked on and improved the cottage, which had been virtually uninhabitable when purchased, so that it could be let out. Mrs Cahill would continue after the divorce to reap the benefit of his efforts.

The court awarded a capital sum of £32,000 to reflect Mr Cahill's efforts.

Maclachlan v Maclachlan (1998). S 9(1)(a) and (c) claims. Donalda Maclachlan sued her husband, Thomas, for divorce. The children were to stay with her. The main asset was the matrimonial home, which was jointly owned, but there were other items of matrimonial property and Donalda owned more than Thomas. Both Donalda and Thomas sought financial provision from the other: he sought a 50% split of the other items of matrimonial property (s 9(1)(a)); she sought a capital sum to help her purchase a house for herself and the children and to help her pay the school fees of the children (s 9(1)(c)).

The court held that it was not appropriate to make a capital sum to cover revenue expenses such as school fees, so that claim was left out of account. Thomas's claim to a share of the matrimonial property was valid; so was Donalda's claim for a share of the costs of bringing up the children. But the value of each claim was roughly the same and so cancelled each other out. No order for financial provision was made to either party.

Loudon v Loudon (1994). S 9(1)(a) and (d) claims. Alison
Loudon sued her husband, Gavin Loudon, for divorce. They had
been married for 17 years and Mrs Loudon had not worked since
the birth of the child of the marriage. The matrimonial property
amounted to £830,000; Mr Loudon was earning around £58,000
per annum net of tax and Mrs Loudon was earning nothing.

The court held that, to reflect Mrs Loudon's contributions to
the marriage (looking after the house and the child and relieving
Mr Loudon of these responsibilities so that he could advance his
own career) she should receive 55% of the matrimonial property;
and that in addition she should receive a periodical allowance of
£500 a month for two years to allow her to be retrained for the job
market.

Haughan v Haughan (2002). A s 9(1)(e) claim. Kathleen Haughan
sued her husband for divorce and as financial provision she sought
payment of a periodical allowance under s 9(1)(e) of the Family
Law (Scotland) Act 1985. This permits a periodical allowance to
be ordered if this is necessary to avoid serious financial hardship.
Mrs Haughan was 51 years old, had been married for 27 years and
during all that time had been dependent on her husband: she was
the homemaker and the parties had lived in some comfort. Since
the separation she had received no aliment from her husband, was
dependent on state benefit, and was of poor health: her chances
of employment were very low. Mr Haughan, on the other hand,
enjoyed good health and earned around £74,000 a year, with an
excess of income over expenditure of some £12,000 per year. The
Lord Ordinary awarded Mrs Haughan a periodical allowance of
£1,000 per month.

Mr Haughan then lost his job and he sought a variation of this
award to nil. He had in the interim paid Mrs Haughan nothing. The
Inner House held that there had been a change in circumstances but
that he could still afford to pay his ex-wife something. A periodical
allowance of £500 per month was substituted for the original
award.

Banks v Banks (2005). Mr and Mrs Banks married in 1965 and,
though two children were born of the marriage, Mr Banks took little
part in family life. The parties stopped sharing a bedroom in 1988. In

1993, Mr Banks took up a new job overseas and thereafter he seldom spent more than two weeks a year with his family. He continued to support them. In 1994 Mrs Banks and the children visited him for a holiday abroad and she might have shared a hotel room with him. In 1997 Mr Banks moved back to the UK, but not back to the family home; he continued to spend large amounts of work time overseas. In 1998 Mr and Mrs Banks had a meeting to discuss the future financial arrangements between the two of them. They ate their last meal together in 2001. In 2003 Mr Banks informed his wife that he would not be returning to her. They divorced in 2005. The question before the court was: when was the "relevant date" (that is, the date of final separation) which was essential for valuing the matrimonial property for financial provision? The property (most of which was in the name of Mr Banks) had increased in value over the years and so it was in Mrs Banks' interests that the relevant date be as late as possible and in Mr Banks' interests that the relevant date be as early as possible. She argued for 2003 when she was informed that he was not coming back, he for 1993 when he had decided in his own mind that the marriage was effectively dead.

The court held that the separation occurred somewhere in between these two dates and considered that the financial meeting in 1998 was significant as a change in the nature of the relationship between the parties. It held that they had separated from that date and so the date of valuation of the matrimonial property was then.

INDEX